Understanding IBM Workplace Strategy & Products

Other Titles of Interest From Maximum Press

More *IBM-Related* Books

- *IBM Software for e-business on demand*
- *IBM On Demand Technology Made Simple*
- *IBM On Demand Technology for the Growing Business*
- *Exploring IBM Server and Storage Technology*
- and many more…

Top e-business Books

- *101 Ways to Promote Your Web Site*
- *Business-to-Business Internet Marketing*
- *Marketing on the Internet*
- and many more…

Special Offers

From IBM and other "*Exploring IBM*" team members

For more information go to *www.maxpress.com/ibmpromo1*
or e-mail us at *moreinfo@maxpress.com*

Understanding IBM Workplace Strategy & Products

Featuring Lotus Workplace

Ron Sebastian

Douglas W. Spencer

MAXIMUM PRESS
605 Silverthorn Road
Gulf Breeze, FL 32561
(850) 934-0819
www.maxpress.com

Publisher: Jim Hoskins

Manager of Finance/Administration: Joyce Reedy

Production Manager: Gina Cooke

Cover Designer: Lauren Smith

Copyeditor: Publication Services

Proofreader: Jacquie Wallace

Indexer: Susan Olason

Printer: P.A. Hutchison

Library of Congress Cataloging-in-Publication Data

Sebastian, Ron, 1956-
Spencer, Douglas (Douglas W.), 1964-
Understanding the IBM workplace strategy & products : people productivity in the on demand business / Ron Sebastian & Douglas Spencer.
p. cm.
ISBN 1-931644-29-2 (pbk. : alk. paper)
1. IBM software. 2. Management information systems. 3. Business—Computer programs. 4. Electronic commerce. I. Sebastian, Ron, 1956- II. Title.
HF5548.38.I26S64 2005
381'.450053—dc22
2004026705

Dedicated to our loving wives:

Gayle Sebastian

and

Kathleen Spencer

Disclaimer

Trademarks

Foreword

The history of collaboration software began with the shift from "office automation equipment" of the 1960s and 1970s as typewriters became word processors, calculators became spreadsheets, and overhead projectors and transparencies were replaced with graphics software packages. These personal productivity tools ushered in an era of explosive growth for the information industry as they became one of the initial justifications for putting personal computers in offices and on everyone's desk. In the late 1980s as this software began to become commonplace in offices, the next wave of collaboration software began as traditional office printed memoranda crossed the chasm into what we now refer to as "e-mail." In fact, e-mail itself was really made possible with the introduction of another hardware capability—local area networks. As the personal computers now populating the modern office became interconnected, e-mail systems really started to link everyone together and increase the speed of business. These personal productivity tools delivered a major productivity push across modern enterprises as we entered the early 1990s.

It was about this time that second generation collaboration platforms began to emerge. A new software category was emerging taking advantage of these newly interconnected personal computer networks—a concept called groupware. As personal productivity began to increase, the next natural extension was to focus in the productivity of "teams." New e-mail systems emerged that started to integrate the tools of the previous generation by adding word processing capabilities directly into e-mail clients, and allowing teams to distribute, review, comment and return documents using a new capability that allowed users to "attach" files from the personal productivity tools to their e-mail. The speed of business began to accelerate. These new groupware systems were initially defined by products like Lotus Notes that really pushed the boundaries of these systems by allowing new classes of applications to be developed quickly and executed across this interconnected environment within an enterprise. New add-on capabilities started to emerge around workflow and document management.

As the industry finally got around to agreeing on open standards as the interconnect architecture for business, and the decades old Internet finally gained a personality with new graphical interfaces (Internet browsers), the boundaries of team productivity software began to extend rapidly. Internet standards were grafted into the existing client/server systems of the earlier part of the decade and enterprises began exchanging information between the customers, their supply chain partners and in some cases, even their competitors. This new interconnect again increased the speed of business. And new tools started to emerge allowing teams to quickly set up Web-based team rooms for sharing both within and beyond their own borders. Newer tools still allowed individuals to start instantly communicating with each other using instant messaging.

As technologies continued to evolve, and new standards began to emerge, continued stress was placed on the existing infrastructures as they continued to mature. Companies were faced with enormous tasks of integrating technologies from multiple vendors and multiple generations. In fact, integration slowly became the toughest challenge that most companies faced as they tried to evolve their infrastructures to support the demands of increasing interconnect, multi-company communication and teaming and seamless supply chains crossing industry ecosystems.

This brings us to the current challenge—integration. And it also opens the door to opportunity. How will the industry respond? What new capabilities will emerge? How can enterprises increase interconnectivity, leverage existing investments and take advantage of emerging technologies? These are the challenges and opportunities that we have taken on with a major initiative within IBM. And that is what this book is about.

IBM Workplace is the beginning of what we believe will be the third generation of collaboration systems. A new platform is emerging that will enable enterprises to evolve their infrastructures (instead of rip and replace) into a modern architecture capable of withstanding the demands of the toughest business challenges.

As we contemplated this new system, we began to look to what worked in the past. First of all, this new system had to enable all of the personal productivity capabilities of the earlier systems—both through seamless integration with existing productivity tools like Microsoft Office, and with the inclusion of new component-based productivity tools for both the Web and rich client environments. Secondly, all of the familiar groupware capabilities needed to exist... e-mail, forms-based applications using workflow, document management, team rooms and the emerging needs around e-learning. And most importantly, these capabilities needed to be reformed or recast into a modern architecture based on open standards. Why? Because we believe that through the definition and expansion of open standards the toughest challenges of integration can be approached in a sensible and cost effective manner.

Once the basic building blocks are in place—componentized, standardized and organized into a consistent platform—then the real work can begin. The goal of the IBM Workplace initiative is not simply to re-implement the existing capabilities, but instead to enable these new capabilities through a new, template-based programming model. A model that allows customers to assemble "composite applications" using standards-based building blocks, extending them easily using a new generation of development tools targeting an unprecedented level of usability. End users, administrators and professional programmers will be able to easily create new components that can seamlessly interact with the capabilities of the system.

It is through this new system that we believe enterprises will be able to tackle the most difficult problems that they face in an increasing on demand world. The ability to quickly bring together the necessary capabilities, both included with the system and those from a rapidly expanding ecosystem, will provide the basis for attacking the integration problems that face every organization. And by creating tools that allow easy introduction of existing technologies into this new model, we believe that enterprises can fully leverage their existing investments in both collaborative and transactional systems.

This book by Ron and Doug will help explain these concepts in more detail and will help you understand how to make that next step into the future of collaboration.

Michael D. Rhodin
Vice President, Lotus Software
IBM Corporation

Table of Contents

Chapter 5: Industry Solutions 100

Introduction

As the IBM software strategy has been executed during the past several years, we've now reached a point of convergence and breakthrough. Breakthroughs usually occur when a combination of factors converge to enable dramatic and new possibilities. The multiyear plans of the IBM software organization have been to develop components, leverage open standards, and focus on building the best in industry middleware software.

The IBM Workplace strategy and products are a breakthrough approach to implementing an IT software infrastructure that not only will better address the needs of the traditional requirements and users, but also enable organizations to reach the nontraditional user community with a cost-appropriate and flexible rich user experience.

This book is intended to provide an executive review of the IBM Workplace strategy and products, with a focus on the Lotus Workplace products. Ron and Doug have combined knowledge and experiences to illustrate the various products within the IBM Workplace family.

Chapter 1 discusses the overall strategy and introduces the new technology platforms and the four product families that fit within the overall IBM Workplace umbrella of solutions. The overall IBM Workplace portfolio includes products from the WebSphere Portal family, the Lotus Domino family, the WebSphere Everyplace family, and the Lotus Workplace family.

Chapter 2 discusses the overall IBM Workplace model of implementation. The IBM Workplace implementation model provides a great, flexible, scalable, and secure foundation. Understanding the way the implementation is structured will help people realize the true value of this approach.

Chapter 3 introduces each of the major and currently available software products from the Lotus Workplace family.

Chapter 4 discusses how technology provided within the Workplace family is enabling a new approach to collaboration, which will bring about changes and breakthroughs in organizational productivity.

IBM delivers many industry solutions built upon the IBM middleware products, such as IBM Workplace. Chapter 5 discusses various industries and example IBM software solutions that are available.

IBM's development and new-product release cycle for the IBM Workplace products is aggressive relative to those of other vendors in the marketplace. New product releases for many of the products are planned to occur on an average of every 6 to 12 months. This is enabled by the component-based development approach that IBM software has adopted. The "server-managed client" model of the IBM Workplace implementation also enables the deployment of new product functions to be fast and relatively easy. Of course, this is all great stuff. But, considering how long it takes to write a book and publish it, we encourage you to consider this book as an introduction to the concepts and example solutions. Please refer to the IBM software Web sites for the latest product announcements and information (*www.ibm.com/software*).

Your "Members Only" Web Site

The IBMWorkplace world changes every day. That's why there is a companion Web site associated with this book. On this site you will find updates to the book and other resources of interest. However, you need a user ID and password to access this site.

To get into the "members only" section of the companion Web site, go to the Maximum Press Web site located at *www.maxpress.com* and follow the links to the companion Web site for this book. When you try to enter, you will be asked for a user ID and password. Type the following:

- For your user ID, enter: *Workplace*
- For you password, enter: *MRE*

You will then be granted full access to the "members only" area. Visit the site often and enjoy the updates and resources with our compliments—and thanks again for buying the book. We ask that you not share the user ID and password for this site with anyone else.

1

Introducing IBM® Workplace™

In any industry, there are occasions when a disruptive technology comes into the market and changes the game. Clayton M. Christensen was the first to coin the term *disruptive technology* as referring to a product of lower cost and performance that gains a foothold in the low end of the market but then progressively moves up with increased capabilities, eventually displacing the incumbent product. Possible examples might include e-books versus paper books, open source versus proprietary, automated teller machines versus the traditional bank teller, digital cameras versus film cameras, or the Internet protocols versus proprietary networks. IBM Workplace is changing the way in which applications are delivered to the end user and will eventually displace the traditional client/server model.

The IBM Workplace family is a pure manifestation of the IBM software strategy as it relates to embracing the On Demand Business™ vision of IBM. The IBM Workplace is an environment that enables dynamic integration of modular components. It also extends the server-based computing model to a rich client that allows for the distribution and management of client-based applications, thus providing a flexible delivery model with a more cost effective implementation compared with traditional client/server.

The IBM Workplace products and strategy embrace the IBM vision for enabling an On Demand Business. The IBM software strategy is well illustrated by IBM Workplace. In this chapter, we will summarize the IBM vision for becoming an On Demand Business and the IBM software strategy. For a deeper discussion about these two important topics, we encourage you to read the book titled *IBM Software for e-business on demand* (ISBN 1-931644-17-9), written by Douglas W. Spencer, (co-author of this book).

IBM's On Demand Business Vision

As illustrated in Figure 1.1, IBM Chairman and CEO Sam Palmisano has defined an On Demand Business as being "an enterprise whose business processes—integrated end-to-end across the company and with key partners, suppliers, and customers—can respond with speed to any customer demand, market opportunity, or external threat." An On Demand Business requires optimization horizontally across its business processes and across those of its business partners and suppliers.

As illustrated in Figure 1.2, there are two key imperatives to becoming an On Demand Business, and our discussion on these will be expanded. The first imperative is innovating the business to differentiate and capture the new value. The second imperative is improving the productivity of resources deployed. These imperatives help drive the business transformations.

The first major insight that IBM recognized is the need for flexibility and innovation in the way you do business. This involves forcing organizations to become more "componentized"—that is, to break down the overall business into the pieces (or components) that make it up. This allows a business to stop

Figure 1.1. Defining an On Demand Business.

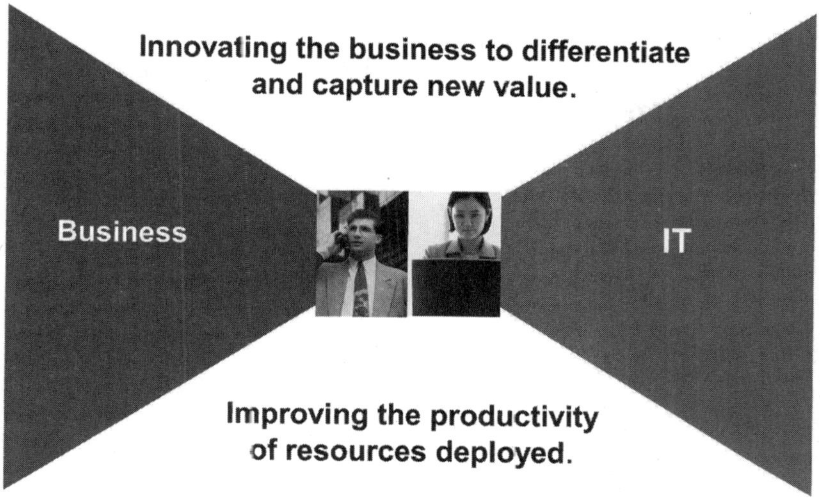

Figure 1.2. Imperatives in today's world.

looking at itself through such lenses as organization, geography, and product or customer segment and instead to start looking at itself through the lenses of discrete functions and processes.

Secondly, there is a stronger linkage between the business model and the supporting IT infrastructure; thus, applications evolve on paths similar to those of the business and thereby become increasingly modular. So instead of focusing on big monolithic applications that are made up of millions of lines of code, organizations are beginning to think about discrete modular elements of application functionality that can more easily be modified as the needs of the business change. As illustrated in Figure 1.3, new business designs are enabled by technology.

Productivity gains do not occur in a straight line rising upward. As illustrated in Figure 1.4, productivity gains occur over time, with periods of moderate or no gain, and then periods of dramatic gain. The dramatic productivity gains usually occur with the maturity and convergence of a mix of technologies and related activities. Related activities include education, awareness, experience, your business partner's adoption of standards, people adopting new technologies, and new ways of doing business. Planning, preparing, and building toward this convergence is the key to achieving the dramatic gains early in the cycle.

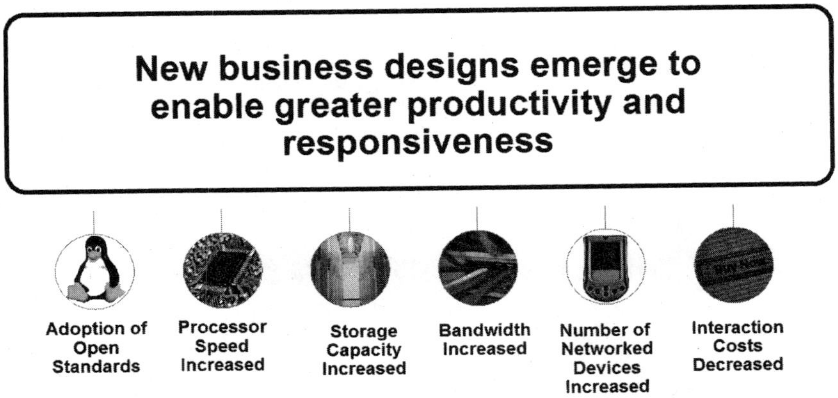

Figure 1.3. Breakthoughs are enabled by technology.

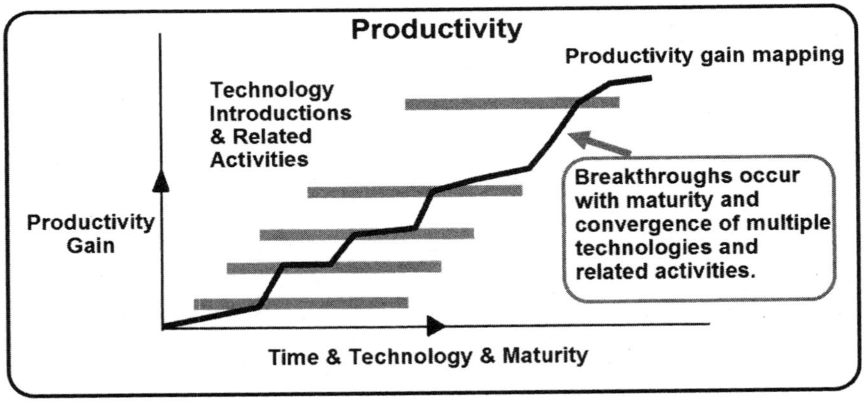

Figure 1.4. Achieving productivity breakthroughs.

Integration across divisions of a business enables the potential for business process breakthroughs. A modular approach to the infrastructure (software and server) design provides the flexibility necessary to have processes built for change.

IBM's Software Strategy

IBM's software division is the world's largest provider of middleware and the second largest software business in the world. It contributes about 15 percent of IBM's total revenue and about one-third of IBM's profits. The IBM Software Group has over 40,000 employees. The Software Group works with 90,000 business partners worldwide, with more than 100 strategic ISV (Independent Software Vendors) alliances. It has 30 software research labs worldwide; 24 on demand software centers; and 14,000 employees dedicated to open software technologies, including Linux, Java, and XML.

The goal of the IBM software strategy is to enable the On Demand Business requirements, such as improving productivity and enabling business agility.

As illustrated in Figure 1.5, IBM Software has embraced IBM's On Demand Business vision by enabling the On Demand Operating Environment with business solutions and IT infrastructure solutions. The overall goal of the IBM Software Group is to provide a complete and specialized portfolio of best-in-industry middleware to accelerate the execution of business strategy and the delivery of business value.

As illustrated in Figure 1.6, the five brands of IBM Software enable a middleware environment that runs across multiple platforms and enabling business applications. The Rational® brand organization provides the development solutions to help enable a reliable software development platform that make it easier for organizations to build software tailored to their business needs. WebSphere® builds software for business application foundations, such as Web application servers and transaction management, and software to support a Services Oriented Architecture, such as an enterprise services bus. Lotus® fun-

Figure 1.5. IBM software strategy.

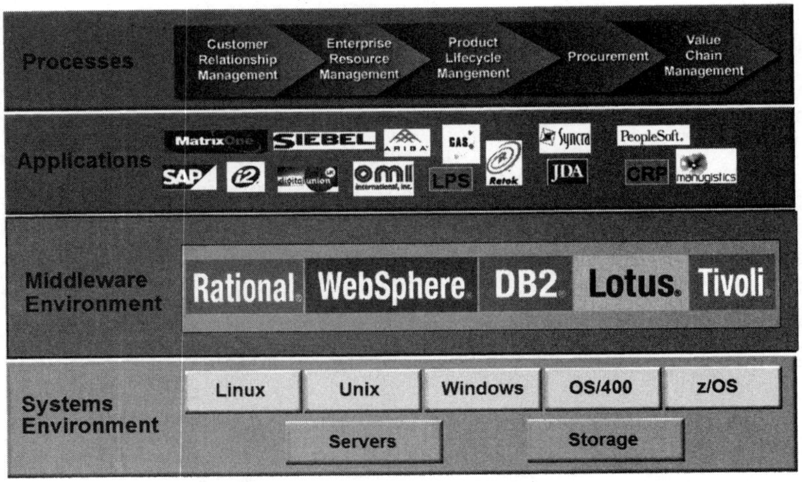

Figure 1.6. IBM software is about Middleware.

damentally changes the way people work together, making possible "intelligent" access to the personal expertise and interactions that drive business results, such as solutions to empower people to collaborate, learn, and team. DB2® information management software provides the information infrastructure for integrating vast amounts of information from a variety of sources, business intelligence offerings that identify trends in data for decision making, and content management offerings to help manage digital media and information assets. Tivoli® provides solutions to help customers automate, secure, and manage IT systems with offerings that can help provide insight to manage the business impact of what occurs throughout IT systems and to orchestrate the right responses.

Open Technology Model

IBM believes that open standards (see Figure 1.7) are essential and will help enable an On Demand Business. By using these standards, organizations are better able to rapidly incorporate products and technologies. IBM supports many IT industry standards such as HTML (a standard that describes how content

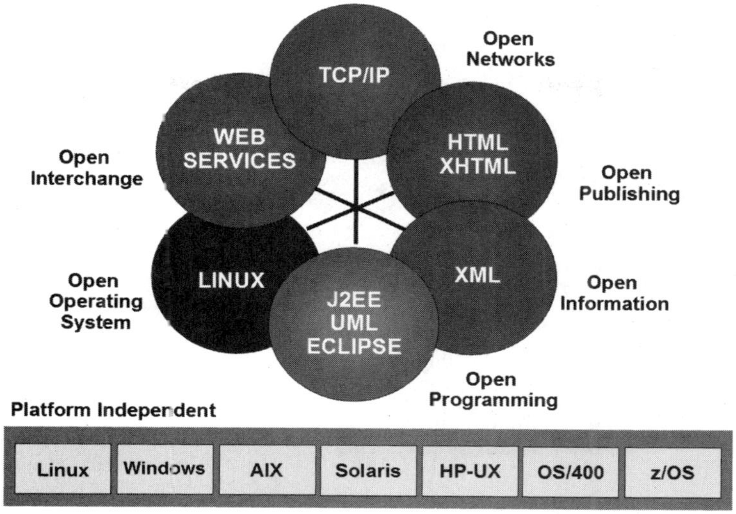

Figure 1.7. IBM software embraces an Open Technology Model.

looks to the user), Java (a programming language that will run on any platform), Java 2 Enterprise Edition (J2EE) (a Java programming specification), open source (a community-based marketplace for software that includes Linux and Eclipse), XML (Extensible Markup Language, which describes data so that it can move between applications), UML (Unified Modeling Language) (a language that simplifies the complex process of software design), Web Services (enabling dynamic business capabilities), and SOA (Service Oriented Architecture).

Service Oriented Architecture

IBM software strategy embraces the Service Oriented Architecture (SOA). As illustrated in Figure 1.8, Service Oriented Architecture enables distributed computing, thus treating software resources as services available on a network through an enterprise service bus. With this, an organization can abstract its IT infrastructure so that it presents its functionality in the form of services that can be accessed independently of the underlying technology that supports them. Service Oriented Architecture is a natural evolution of industry standards such

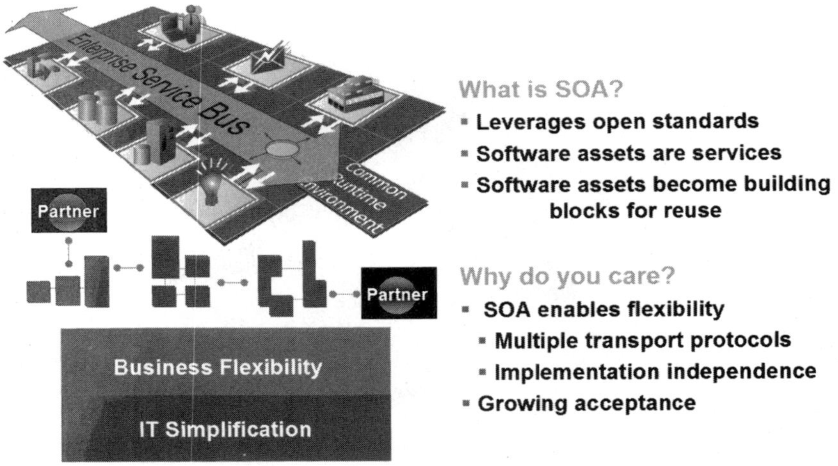

Figure 1.8. IBM software embraces Service Oriented Architecture.

as Web Services and middleware. It is now widely viewed as the architecture for the next wave of computing.

Componentization

IBM's software strategy is to deliver leadership capabilities through the five brand organizations. Each brand organization has the mission to develop software that is platform independent, scalable, modular, standards based, reliable, and globalized for flexible integration into heterogeneous environments. This is a strategy of building components, rather than just products, which is good for IBM, IBM Business Partners building solutions, and most importantly it is better for customers that implement IBM Software-based solutions because it enables flexibility.

Each brand focuses on its areas of expertise. Rational is focused on solutions for the lifecycle of software development. Tivoli is building solutions for security, system management, and automation. WebSphere builds Web application servers, transaction management, and business integration. DB2 is focused on information management. Lotus builds software for collaboration. While building software for a focus area, each brand builds modular components that

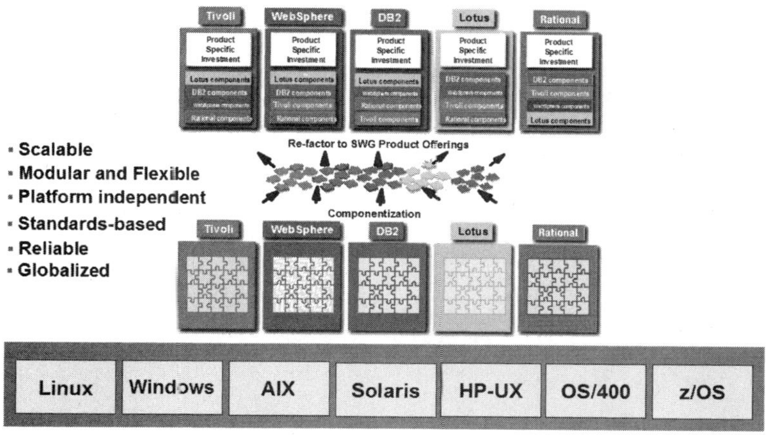

Figure 1.9. IBM software is about building shared components.

can be shared with the other brands. As illustrated in Figure 1.9, IBM software strategy is about building and sharing components so that IBM leverages technology more effectively and rapidly increases the development/delivery time line for new products. This part of the strategy is demonstrated well in products such as WebSphere Portal and the Lotus Workplace Solutions.

What is IBM Workplace?

For the purposes of this discussion, the overall IT software infrastructure is described in three high-level segments, as illustrated in Figure 1.10. In the back end, there is all that is required to support traditional middleware functions of business process management and information management. The third segment addresses the front end, which incorporates a set of services that users need for collaboration and integration with the back end. This third segment also includes the mechanisms that deliver those applications to the various types of users. IBM Workplace is a family of products and technologies that addresses this front end requirement.

The whole notion of IBM Workplace is to be able to extend out to the things that customers work on—whether it be their desktops, laptops, or mobile devices—a complete computing environment that allows them to interact seamlessly with all the applications that they would want to use within the

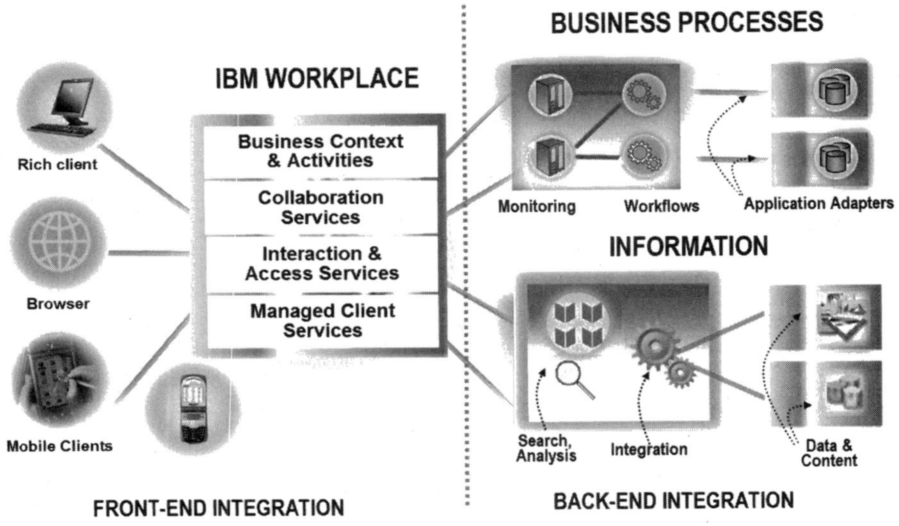

Figure 1.10. IBM Workplace extends back end services to users.

company they work with or even out on the Internet. What IBM has done is to take a lot of the core technologies that have been delivered on the server side, such as the WebSphere environment, and to extend them down onto different devices. IBM has taken elements of its software, shrunk them down from a size perspective, so that everything from PDAs to laptops or desktops are enabled with an entirely consistent environment. Workplace is a fully mobile environment. People can take their work with them, and, when they connect, their work can synchronize back up to the server. Everything that comes down to the desktop is controlled through the server environment.

Workplace provides an environment rich with security features. IBM has built around this environment an extensive set of capabilities for mail, calendar, address book, discussion databases, instant messaging, integrated messaging for voice over IP, learning, team workspaces, and Web conferencing. There are also things such as a document management capability for editing documents, spreadsheets, and graphics.

Workplace offers a variety of client "weights." IBM is not advocating only thick or thin clients. The Workplace environment allows users to operate a thin client with full function, such as a browser. Or, a user can move their work down to a client environment for improved performance; the mobility and synchronization capabilities enable disconnected client support as well. Workplace is an entirely portable environment because Workplace operates on Windows, Linux, and the Mac operating systems.

IBM Workplace Strategy

The IBM Workplace strategy is aimed at defining and delivering the services required to integrate the user to the back-end business process and information infrastructures, thus creating a new level of business productivity. IBM Workplace defines a server-managed client model in which user experiences of differing levels (from simple browser to rich client) can be delivered based on the various end-user requirements. The strategy is also about enabling a "game-changing" way for the user community to interact more productively and at a cost that allows a business or organization to extend these services not only to the traditional users (e.g., information workers with a desktop PC), but also to nontraditional users (general non-office employees).

The game-changing aspect of this approach is that now everyone in an organization can participate in the new era of computing, which will dramatically enhance organizational effectiveness. Examples of nontraditional users are flight attendants, bank tellers, manufacturing plant floor workers, nurses, doctors, city maintenance staff, and school teachers. The cost of providing these types of users traditional rich client applications, e-mail, and user services, had been prohibitive. Now, with the IBM Workplace family of products (such as Lotus Workplace), it is affordable to provide rich user functions, including e-mail, document editing, HR applications, etc. By affordable, we mean doing all that and more (such as electronic pay stubs for less per year than the cost of mailing paper-based pay stubs).

IBM Workplace

With the IBM Workplace, IBM is providing a vast array of capabilities that can be suited to individual business needs. The capabilities extend from the back end, where IBM has long provided the middleware for business integration, application development, and information management, to the front end, where the user interaction takes place.

Simply put, IBM Workplace is a family of products and technologies that help deliver server-managed clients of choice, supporting multiple user types and end-user experiences and across a wide range of access points and forms of connectivity, thus enabling a flexible and cost-effective collaborative access for people, business processes, applications, and content.

Looking at the stack of IBM Workplace services illustrated in Figure 1.10 (front-end integration), we see a set of reusable components that can be applied based on the organization's or on individual users' needs. IBM Workplace provides these four layers (or categories) of component-based services that can be applied according to a business's need to integrate with the back-end services.

The first layer in the stack is a set of components for business context and activities, such as messaging (e-mail) components, regulatory compliance components, enterprise resource planning, application infrastructure components, and so on.

The second layer consists of the collaborative services, which include calendaring, Team Spaces, learning, instant messaging, and document management. Essentially, all of the collaborative services organizations need to integrate people into their business, or business processes.

The third layer is the interaction and access services layer, which includes technology components to support portal-based services (access to applications, personalization, customization, etc.) and necessary connectivity services for mobile devices. These connections with other people are made through personalized integrated access to what people need to do their jobs, based on their roles.

The fourth layer comprises managed client services, which provide the services necessary to deliver the appropriate user experience. This includes support for browser-based access to applications, mobile client environment, and a new rich client environment. The rich client environment provides an infrastructure that delivers the rich user experience normally found only in the traditional client/server architecture, but with the total cost of ownership (TCO) of a browser-based implementation.

IBM Workplace is a model for delivering rich user applications to a broad range of devices and usages, all from the server. This delivers the richness of client/server with the cost characteristics and no-touch deployment of the browser model.

The managed client model means that businesses, organizations, and business partners can extend many existing applications, or build new ones, that can deliver clients of choice: the broad spectrum of user interaction, all with centralized deployment and management. This model is for delivering rich user applications to a broad range of devices and usages all from the server.

IBM Workplace is a "game changer" which many companies are embracing. Companies like Siebel, Adobe, PeopleSoft, Research In Motion (RIM with Blackberry), and Relavis have been working with IBM as early adopters of this model.

IBM has a phenomenal portfolio of products and services that no competitor can match. IBM has the power of one architectural model, one programming model, and one consistent tool—and all standards based. This enables flexible and cost-effective access to people, business processes, applications, and content.

IBM Workplace Products

With the various names, announcements, and communications surrounding the products discussed in this book, it can be confusing to understand what the actual products are as distinguished from the relevant technologies. There are technology components and there are actual products delivered to the market. The two main technologies delivered in the IBM Workplace portfolio are called IBM Workplace Client Technology, Rich Edition, and the IBM Workplace Client Technology, Micro Edition.

As illustrated in Figure 1.11, there are four product families that fit within the IBM Workplace portfolio, namely the Lotus Notes®/Domino® family, the

Figure 1.11. IBM Workplace family of products.

WebSphere Portal family, the Lotus Workplace family, and the WebSphere Everyplace family. As mentioned earlier in this chapter, IBM Workplace strategy is all about supporting a server-managed client environment, which all of these families of products embrace. For example, WebSphere Portal is the engine that manages a browser interface. In addition to browser support, the Lotus Workplace server also provides server-based management for a connected or disconnected rich client environment.

The Notes/Domino, WebSphere Portal, and WebSphere Everyplace families have existed for some time and will continue to evolve as part of the IBM Workplace strategy and take advantage of the IBM Workplace technologies.

The Lotus Workplace family is relatively new and has three clients: a browser client, a workstation rich client, and a PDA rich client. The Lotus Workplace workstation rich client is based on the IBM Workplace Client Technology, Rich Edition. The Lotus Workplace PDA rich client is based on the IBM Workplace Client Technology, Micro Edition.

Now, having read all the names and families, we are sure you are really confused (smile). But, hang in there, and hopefully by the time you finish reading this book, it will all make sense.

As illustrated in Figure 1.12, one of the goals of the IBM Workplace strategy is to enable rich portal-based applications enhanced with rich user experience. IBM is doing this by designing a system that has the benefits experienced with browser-deployed applications (low cost, open standards-based interface, multi-platform, rapid deployment, etc.) combined with the benefits of a PC-based deployment (disconnected, rich application support, customization, etc).

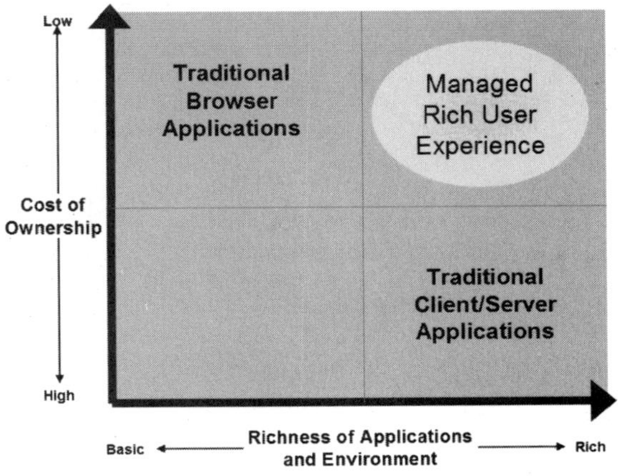

Figure 1.12. Achieving rich client functionality with a low total cost of ownership.

The other aspect to this is providing the benefits without the negatives associated with those environments. Obviously, a browser isn't very functional when disconnected. A traditional PC-based environment is costly, difficult to maintain, more prone to viruses, etc. The Workplace environment provides a low-cost, managed, and rich user experience.

When we (Ron and Doug) began in the computer industry, there were still a lot of applications built that were written directly to the hardware devices, which was very difficult and required highly technical skills. As operating systems (OS) appeared on the market, it became easier for developers to build applications using the application programming interfaces (APIs) of the OS. But, the real explosion of applications that were being built began when middleware was introduced, making it even easier for people to build applications. Middleware could be a database engine or a collaboration environment. As middleware such as DB2 and Lotus Notes/Domino appeared, it became much easier for new applications to be built and deployed by business professionals. Tools such as Domino Designer made it really easy for even business professionals to develop reliable business applications and deploy them to users in a client/server model. As illustrated in Figure 1.13, the advantages expe-

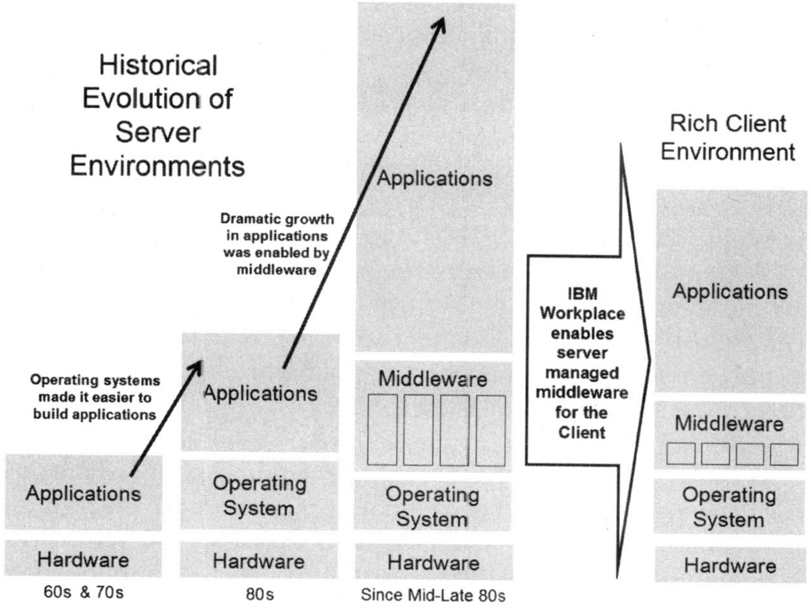

Figure 1.13. Middleware enables new applications.

rienced on the server with middleware are being enabled now in a server-managed client environment so that there is a reliable middleware platform on the client with the introduction of IBM Workplace Technologies. This cross-platform middleware with a component-based model and new easy-to-design tooling should enable yet another explosion of new applications.

IBM Workplace Client Technology, Rich Edition

IBM Workplace Client, Rich Edition is not a product, it is an enabling technology. IBM is a major contributor to open standards and has taken a leadership role in the open-source initiative for a rich client framework. Building on the Eclipse open source development environment, IBM has now created a client-side framework for the deployment and management of business applications. This framework, IBM Workplace Client Technology, will help drive the next evolution in network-centric computing.

IBM Workplace Client Technology addresses the growing demand for dynamic, powerful applications (the rich client experience) that can be deployed and managed affordably. Because of the way Workplace Client Technology shares code and processing work among clients and middleware servers, organizations that embrace this technology and the applications built on it will have the flexibility of client-side applications combined with the server-side control and cost savings traditionally associated with Web-based computing. Not only will this be a boon to IT administrators, but also the end user will be able to enjoy the richness of a traditional client with security, fast response time, user interface (UI) consistency, off-line support, and tighter integration with desktop productivity applications.

As illustrated in Figure 1.14, the potential exists for users to access necessary data and applications anytime, anywhere and from any device, with the full functionality of traditional client software. IBM Workplace Client Technology will also provide independent software vendors (ISVs) with an extensible run-time environment, thus opening up major new possibilities for application delivery. It is also the foundation for the rich client versions of the Lotus Workplace family of solutions.

As illustrated in Figure 1.15, the user environment provides a lot of flexibility for the end user in terms of what applications are displayed and how they are managed. The server-managed model enables greater centralized control, while enabling great individual customization. The components deployed and the display are well managed from the server.

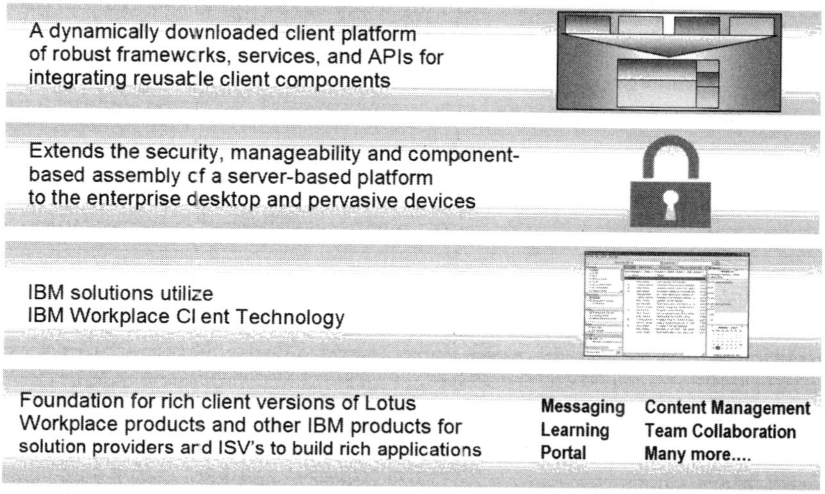

Figure 1.14. IBM Workplace Client Technology platform.

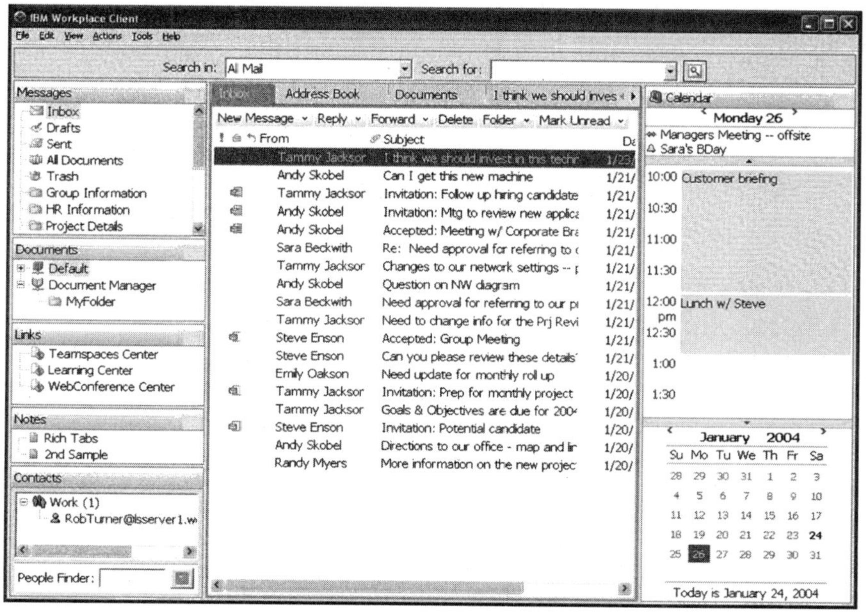

Figure 1.15. IBM Workplace Client Technology, Rich Edition.

IBM Workplace Client Technology, Micro Edition

IBM Workplace Client Technology, Micro Edition extends the rich client model to mobile devices. This is a platform from which the next generation of device applications can be deployed. As a powerful enabler of on demand capabilities, it delivers a Java-powered platform where devices have access to pretested content, can be maintained over-the-air (OTA), and are pre-enabled for access to enterprise data, applications, and transactions. As illustrated in Figure 1.16, the rich user experience can be delivered to PDAs.

The needs and solutions of an on demand world include the end-to-end integration of people, processes, and information within and beyond the enterprise. This can vary dramatically by industry. But for the members of the wireless ecosystem, namely, service providers, carriers, and device manufacturers, giving the mobile enterprise easy and immediate access to information and applications is the key to staying ahead in the wireless game.

This platform for deploying high-value data services on mobile devices to the on demand enterprise provides key functions such as pretested content with proven performance, standards-based middleware to provide a Java 2 Platform, Micro Edition (J2ME) run-time, configurable to address memory and CPU constraints, and a set of integrated tools. This technology is available on multiple platforms and in multiple configurations, supporting application deployment across millions of devices.

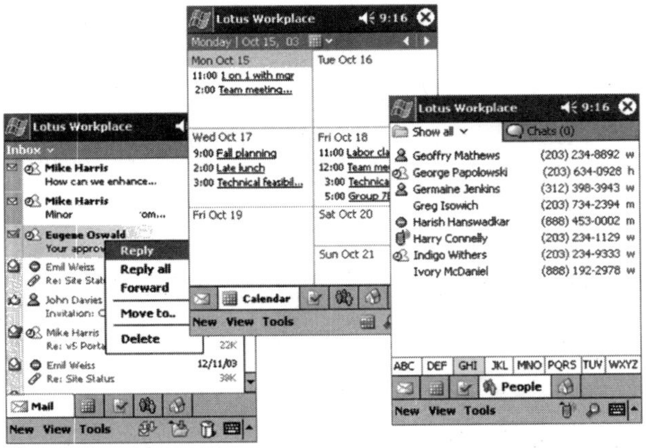

Figure 1.16. IBM Workplace Client Technology, Micro Edition.

Lotus Notes and Domino

The Notes and Domino environment has evolved over 15 years. There are thousands of applications built on Domino. There are over 100 million Notes/Domino users. Domino provides an enterprise level e-mail system, document database model architecture, powerful collaboration server, and reliable client/server model environment. An entire business software environment could be built on the Domino infrastructure, as Domino is a powerful Web application server platform. Lotus Notes continues to set the standard for innovation in the messaging and collaboration market Lotus defined over a decade ago. As an integrated collaborative environment, Lotus Notes combines enterprise-class messaging, calendaring, and scheduling capabilities with a robust platform for collaborative applications.

Lotus Domino

Lotus Domino is a scalable Web application environment that is available on multiple platforms. Domino has a strong history of providing a foundation for business applications to all sizes of organizations. This support has evolved with the times, and Domino's leadership position as an integrated Web application and collaboration server has only strengthened. Lotus Domino provides a foundation for collaboration and business application-logic solutions from corporate messaging to mission-critical Web-based transactions. This enterprise-class messaging and collaboration system is built to improve human productivity by enabling the contribution and expertise of individuals, teams, and extended communities to be utilized. Domino provides industry-leading security. Server availability with Lotus Domino is supported with clustering, transaction logging, server fault recovery, and automated diagnostic tools.

Lotus Domino is a comprehensive application platform for collaboration workflow that handles both connected and disconnected requirements for data and applications. Domino provides a complete infrastructure to create, test, deploy, and manage distributed, multilingual applications. It can facilitate a directory, data, Web applications, Java applications, administration, security, and connectivity, and be a foundation for server-based applications.

Domino began in the client/server era as a powerful document database model collaboration application server and has evolved into the on demand era supporting new approaches to implementing applications, such as Web Services and a Service Oriented Architecture. Lotus Domino can support Java servlets but is not a J2EE platform. J2EE-based applications can be built on the

IBM WebSphere Application Server environment, which integrates easily with the Domino infrastructure.

Domino is a good foundation for building document-centric and workflow process routing applications. Domino is excellent for handling process workflow applications that range from basic to complex, such as project team rooms, document repositories, discussion forums, sales-force enablement, employee self-service, approval-process management, and many other collaborative-workflow business applications. The secure distributed application model of Domino combined with client environments that support Domino (such as Notes and iNotes) enables a mobile workforce to have rich workflow process applications that span servers, clients, different time zones, mobility, and multiple connections to various application systems. Domino is built to support important industry standards such as Web Services and XML.

There are a few additional Domino-based products, such as Lotus Instant Messaging and Web Conferencing (Sametime), Lotus Team Workplace (Quickplace), and Lotus Domino Document Manager.

Domino applications and e-mail environments can be accessed by a user using several client-based environments. Lotus Notes integrates into Domino and provides messaging, collaborative, and PIM resources (e.g., e-mail, calendar, to-do list), and a base to run the client side of Domino applications and databases. Lotus notes can allow people to use these applications whether or not the users are connected with the network.

IBM Lotus Notes and Domino is a well-established platform on which many organizations, large and small, have built substantial numbers of business applications. There are over 100 million Notes users. There are many large enterprises that have implemented thousands of Notes/Domino-based applications and rely on them to run the business. IBM itself has over 10,000 Notes/Domino applications in production and many of those are business-critical applications. Because Domino applications are easily integrated with environments like WebSphere Application Server and WebSphere Portal, the ability to leverage either environment for the respective strengths is made possible. Many people access applications that appear via portlets displayed in the WebSphere Portal environment, but they are actually back-end Domino applications.

One of the main reasons for the explosion of Notes/Domino applications throughout the world is the ability for people to build applications without having to have deep programming skills. Secondly, the reliable replication capability and client/server deployment model allows for the flexibility that many organizations need. A marketing professional, finance person, or any business professional that needs to create an application, can do so with relatively easy-to-use development tools. The deployment of the application is very simple and very reliable. As illustrated in Figure 1.17, Domino Designer enables the building of Notes/Domino applications.

Domino has been significantly enhanced over the years to support the Web Services standards. Using Domino designer, you can now turn Domino applications into Web Services. This allows other systems to access these Domino applications in an industry standards approach and provides better integration of Domino applications with other mission-critical applications.

Domino Designer allows you to consume a Web service and make it part of the Domino application. This provides the ability to better integrate other services within the Domino environment. Since Lotus Workplace is also based on Web Services, the integration of the two products is made easier. A business could decide to continue to use the powerful mail and calendaring functions of Notes/Domino while utilizing the new services of Lotus Workplace in a single user environment.

Users find features that enable collaborative productivity. Application developers find ways to leverage their development skills. Administrators have tools that make it easier to manage the largest collaboration environments.

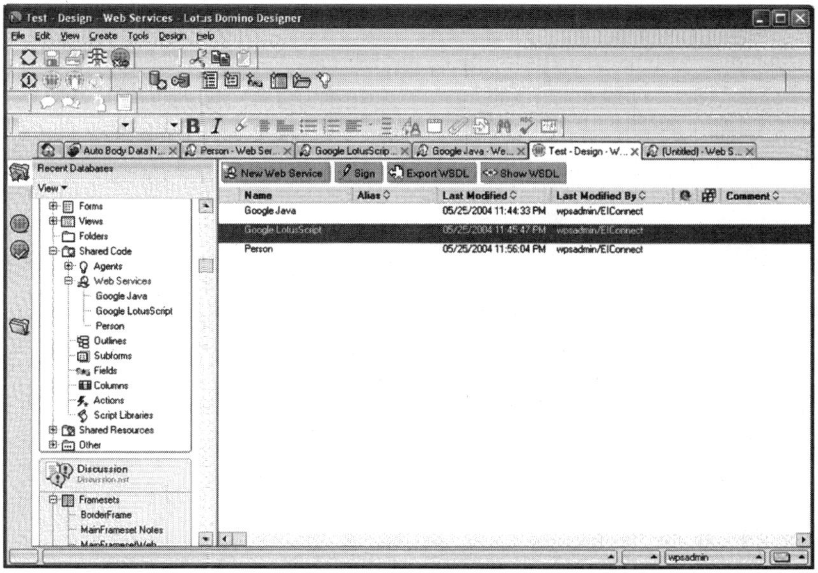

Figure 1.17. Lotus Domino Designer.

Domino provides for scalable, high performance collaboration applications, and has autonomic capabilities. Systems can start small, scale as business needs grow, and provide tools to assist administrators. Domino networks can be large, and typically administrators suffer from too much information, not too little. Domino's autonomic tools consolidate the information so that administrators can use it to make judgments about the health of the network. In some cases, it can even suggest ways to solve or prevent problems, such as moving a workload from one server to another to improve performance.

Collaboration functionality continues to evolve, and starting with Notes/Domino 6.5, users can take advantage of integrated instant messaging and awareness within calendar documents and calendar views. Domino has support for multithreaded views, which let users work on other things while a large view is loading.

Domino provides reliable and highly secure encryption for applications and databases. There is also consistent password management and single sign-on. Plus, consistent password management and installation enables simplified administration and lower administrative costs.

With Notes/Domino, organizations can take advantage of IBM Workplace and IBM Workplace Client Technology. For example, Domino Document Manager adds support for standards common to IBM Workplace, such as the JSR 170 document management standard, and the SIP (Simple Instant Messaging) standard, which enables enterprises to host mixed communities of SIP Simple and Sametime instant messaging users. The Notes plug-in lets any Notes application run with full compatibility and fidelity in applications delivered on Workplace Client Technology, IBM's new platform for enabling rich user experiences via centrally managed clients. This plug-in means someone using IBM Workplace Documents could also use Notes mail, calendaring, and other Notes applications from within that Workplace Client environment.

IBM Lotus Domino Web Access (iNotes) is a sophisticated Web client that gives end users leading Domino messaging and collaboration features that were previously available only with a Lotus Notes client. Domino Web Access (see Figure 1.18) provides the reliability and security features of the IBM Lotus Domino server but delivered through a Web browser. Domino Web Access lets users access Lotus Domino on a Linux server from a Linux desktop, providing a leading-edge, end-to-end collaborative solution for Linux. Domino Web Access provides a browser client to support access to Domino applications via a Web browser, for example, the Mozilla browser on Linux.

As illustrated in Figure 1.19, IBM Lotus Domino Access for Microsoft Outlook (iNotes for Microsoft Outlook) provides advanced functionality within the familiar interface of Microsoft Outlook. This is a collaborative server solution that delivers the leading messaging, calendar, scheduling, and PIM services of Lotus Domino technology to Outlook clients. Lotus Domino Access for Mi-

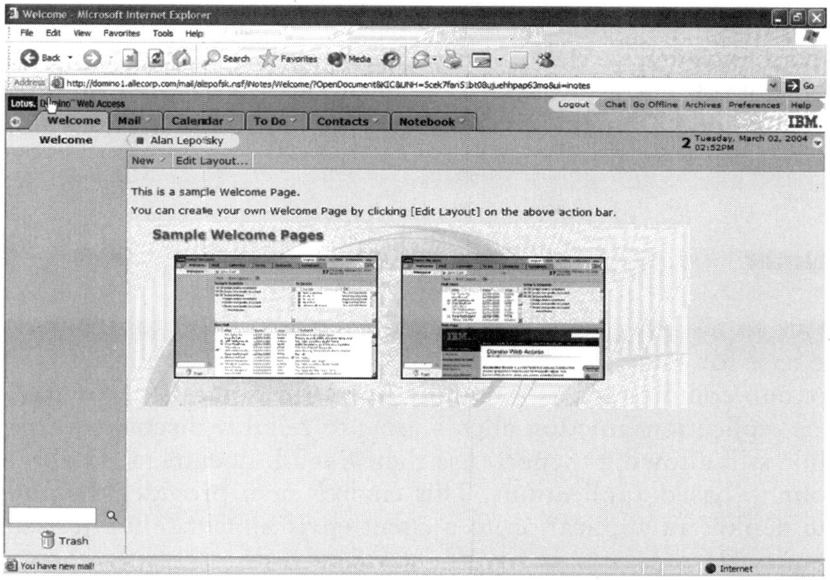

Figure 1.18. Lotus Domino Web Access.

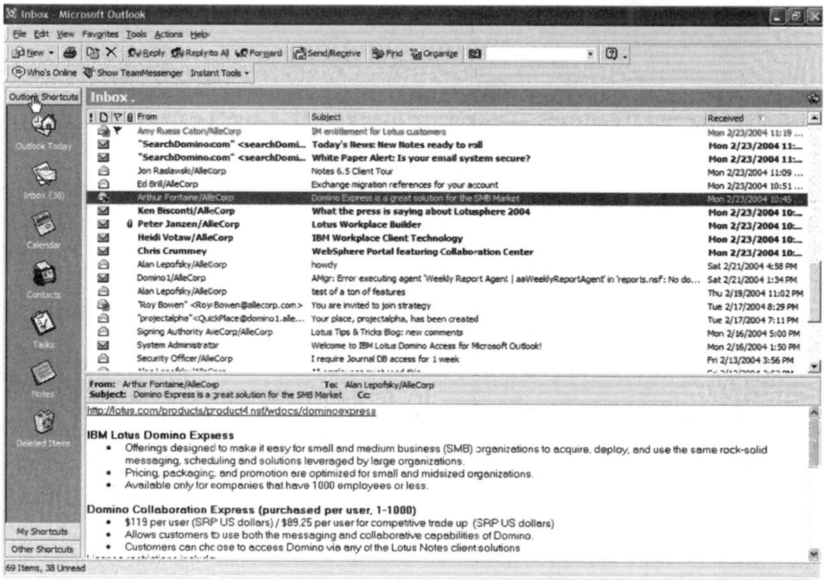

Figure 1.19. Lotus Domino Access for Microsoft Outlook.

crosoft Outlook helps businesses easily and cost-effectively moves from a Microsoft Exchange server to a Lotus Domino server while allowing users to work with Outlook clients, which lets organizations replace Microsoft Exchange servers with Lotus Domino servers to leverage the extensive messaging capabilities provided in Domino.

Lotus Notes

Lotus Notes gives users a single, unified access point for the tools, tasks, and the base for using the client side of Domino-based applications. A Notes and Domino combination is especially powerful in terms of reliable replication. This replication function allows users to reliably disconnect from the server while still allowing them to use their e-mail, document database, and other Domino-based applications. This environment provides the ability to build and deploy an application to a client environment reliably, easily, and with security features.

As illustrated in Figure 1.20, Notes enables a productive collaborative user environment. For example, multithreaded views let you work on other

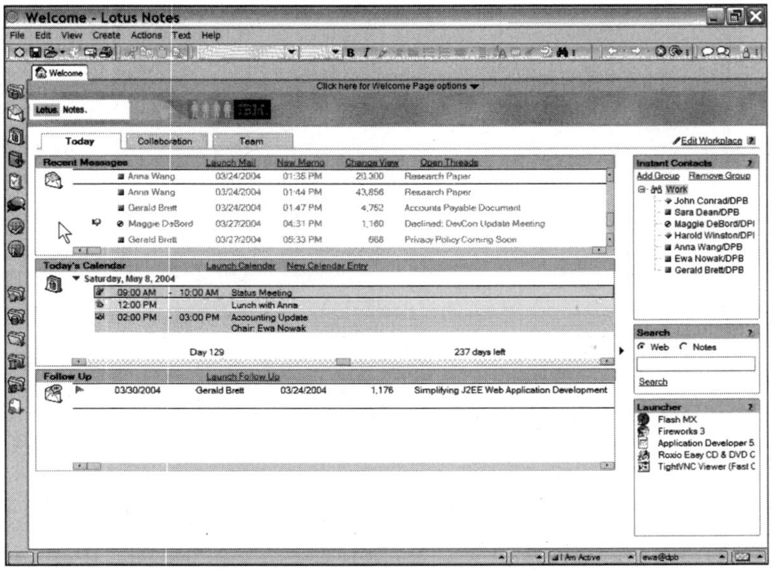

Figure 1.20. Lotus Notes.

things while a large view is loading. A user can sort mail by subject. There is good integration between electronic meetings and calendaring and scheduling so users can manage aspects related to electronic meetings from within the Notes calendar.

Lotus Instant Messaging functionality has been integrated into Notes (starting with Notes 6.5) to provide presence awareness and enable users to initiate chats with colleagues without launching a separate application. This helps maximize responsiveness and ease of use through follow-up function and visual indicators to show users when they have forwarded or replied to e-mail messages. Notes provides calendaring and scheduling functionality, which lets users collaborate and schedule meetings with colleagues across the world.

A future release of Notes is expected to be built using the IBM Workplace Client Technology. Notes, in effect, would become an Eclipse-based plug-in. This would allow the Notes client to break away from its dependence on the Windows operating system and be able to run on the platforms supported by the IBM Workplace Client technology. This will allow one seamless user interface for Domino-based applications and Lotus Workplace applications. The Notes environment has good integration with the rich client of Lotus Workplace currently. With the planned future release of Notes Version 8, it is expected that the Notes client will be delivered fully as the rich client.

WebSphere Portal

Let's begin by defining what a portal is because there are many definitions possible. Firstly, a portal is an aggregation point that will aggregate multiple Web-based applications that a particular user or community of users may need to access in a collective view in a browser environment. As illustrated in Figure 1.21, WebSphere Portal provides this and more capabilities.

This concept for a portal is similar in the way that Windows originally started as an aggregation engine for DOS-based applications, where we could run multiple DOS at the same time. However it was a much different environment when you were running a DOS application under Windows versus running a Windows application. The integration of the applications is much better for Windows applications running in Windows, not because they are different in the functionality of the DOS-based application, but rather that they take advantage of the infrastructure that Windows provides and the DOS application did not. WebSphere Portal is like the windowing environment for the Web.

Secondly, a portal should be more than just an aggregation engine, it needs to be an infrastructure for building applications. A complete set of capabilities

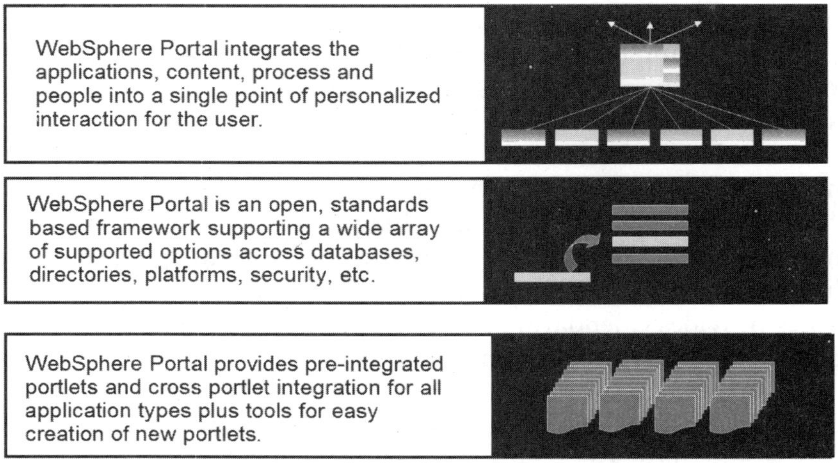

Figure 1.21. WebSphere Portal defined.

and services provided in WebSphere Portal establishes an infrastructure within which developers can write applications. This also provides a much tighter integration between the applications.

IBM WebSphere Portal allows people to interact with applications in a personalized way (see Figure 1.22). They can access the dynamic information they need. They can quickly execute business processes across critical applications. They can collaborate with portal users inside and outside the business. The WebSphere Portal solutions can help organizations improve employee productivity, cut costs, and strengthen relationships with customers and trading partners.

WebSphere Portal helps build scalable and reliable business-to-employee, business-to-business, and business-to-consumer portals. It delivers a single point of personalized interaction with applications, content, processes, and people for a unified user experience, thereby allowing users to view, search, create, convert, and edit basic documents, spreadsheets, and presentations from within the portal. WebSphere Portal provides powerful collaboration capabilities, such as instant messaging, team workplaces, a people finder, and meetings. It enables quick portal integration with back-end systems via portlet builders. WebSphere Portal for multi-platforms is available in two offerings: Portal Enable and Portal Extend.

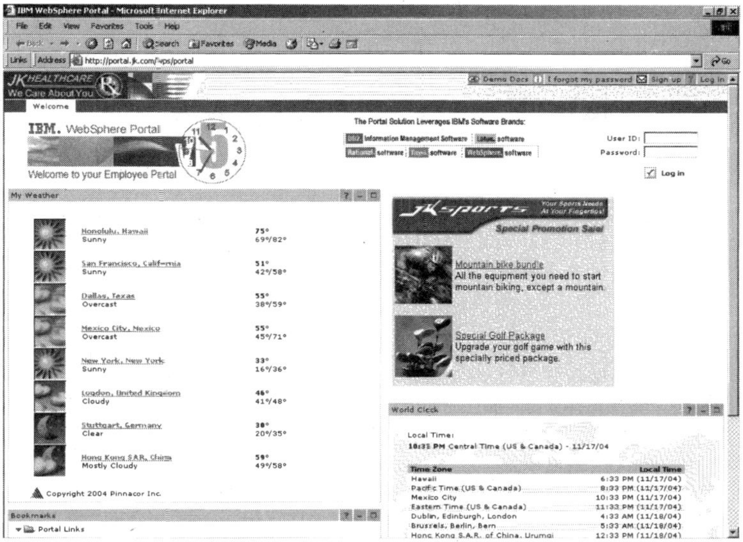

Figure 1.22. WebSphere Portal.

With this portal infrastructure, organizations can build and publish local portlets as remote Web Services or subscribe to Web Services to make them available to portal users via portlets. WebSphere Portal provides C2A (Click2Action) technology for portlet-to-portlet communication and action, ensuring the accuracy of information passed and delivering it on demand. The presentation services allow for the customization of the computing desktop to match individual work patterns and roles. The browser-based content publishing and personalization technology enables users to get a unique experience with the latest information. Portal includes WebSphere Translation Server functionality, which helps users translate the contents of portlets from English to French, Italian, German, Spanish, Portuguese, Taiwanese, Japanese, simplified Chinese, and traditional Chinese, and vice versa.

As illustrated in Figure 1.23, WebSphere Portal also includes Portal Document Manager, which provides a way for portal users to share, view, and organize files of all types—ranging from documents to spreadsheets within the portal community. This communication enhancer offers category subscription services, simple approval processes for file contribution, automatic dialog boxes for contributing Portal search, versioning so that users can track the evolution of a

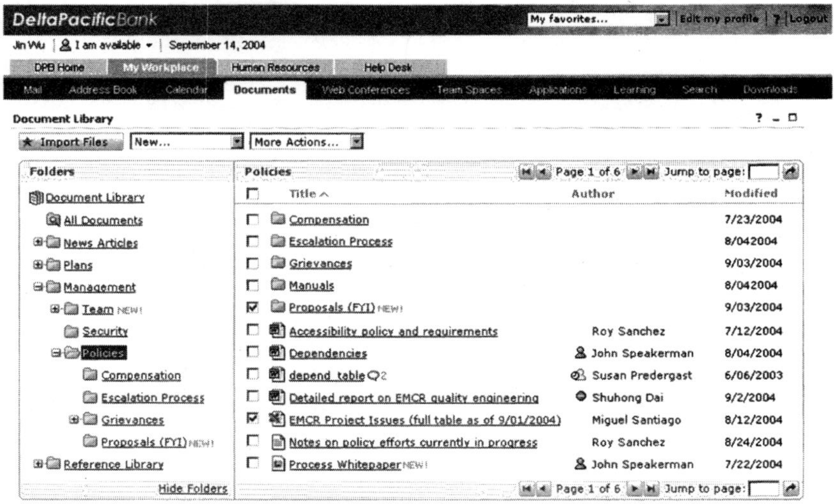

Figure 1.23. WebSphere Portal Document Manager.

piece of content, and access control for managing viewing privileges of different content items. Enable has new productivity components that allow users to view, create, convert, and edit basic documents, spreadsheets, and presentation files from the portal interface. They can therefore execute ad hoc business processes from the same place they access their applications, search for information, and collaborate with other employees and partners. The productivity components are integrated with the document-management feature, so files can be indexed, categorized, and searched by other portal users.

The Portal Application Integrator allows business users to quickly create portlets for interacting with relational databases, Domino databases, and enterprise applications from Oracle, SAP, Siebel, and PeopleSoft. A redesigned installation procedure and improved administration portlets help organizations quickly get a return on their investment while using fewer IT resources. The improved scalability and reliability of WebSphere Application Server provides mission-critical portal services to users.

WebSphere Portal provides functions that help to improve the portal deployment, such as robust Web analysis technology, which provides vital business intelligence about users who interact with the portal environment so that you can continually improve their satisfaction, and extended search capabilities across relational databases such as DB2, Oracle, Lotus Domino databases, Web search engines, and text or HTML documents.

Domino and WebSphere Portal Integration

To provide integration with the Domino family, WebSphere Portal includes the portlets necessary for that integration. This includes portlets for e-mail, instant messaging, Web conferencing, team workplace, and document manager. As illustrated in Figure 1.24, this enables an environment that provides a single integrated view of the Domino collaborative services within, thus leveraging the best of Domino and WebSphere Portal combined.

There are many ways of connecting to Domino data within WebSphere Portal. For example, WebSphere Portal Application Integrator provides a portlet builder that allows basic access to the Domino data. There are also a number of prebuilt portlets so that you can take specific Domino functions and start to integrate them together to make the end user experience much easier. A portlet called the *Domino Web Application Portlet* is a proxy that allows you to grab the input stream as it is coming out of the Domino engine and remap the markup language information so that a Domino Web application operates smoothly within the portal environment.

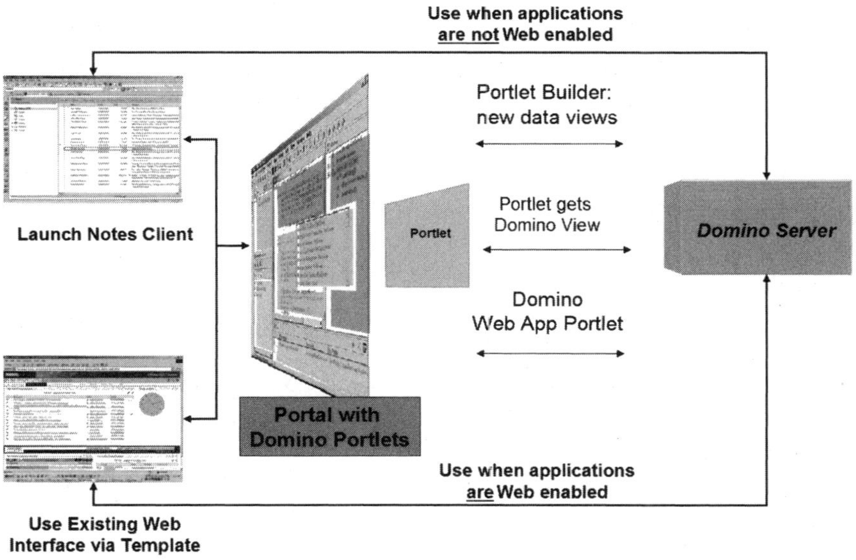

Figure 1.24. Domino Integration with WebSphere Portal.

Lotus Workplace

As illustrated in Figure 1.25, IBM Lotus Workplace (LWP) is an integrated family of collaborative products based on open standards. Lotus Workplace combines market-leading collaborative products that can be experienced through a choice of security-rich clients, giving people simplified access and interaction with other people and a host of collaborative capabilities such as e-mail, calendaring, and scheduling; instant messaging; Web conferencing; team spaces; document and Web content management; and learning.

Lotus Workplace is enabled to deliver a variety of server-managed client experiences ranging from browser based to a new full rich client. The server-managed client model provides administrators a security-rich, no-touch deployment model coupled with central policy-based management of the end user's desktop environment.

IBM® Lotus® Workplace Messaging™ provides a standards-based, simple messaging experience for browser users, while now providing server-managed delivery of a rich client experience for those users who can benefit from an extended set of integrated productivity tools.

IBM Lotus Workplace Team Collaboration provides an integrated instant messaging and presence awareness, Web conferencing, and customizable Team

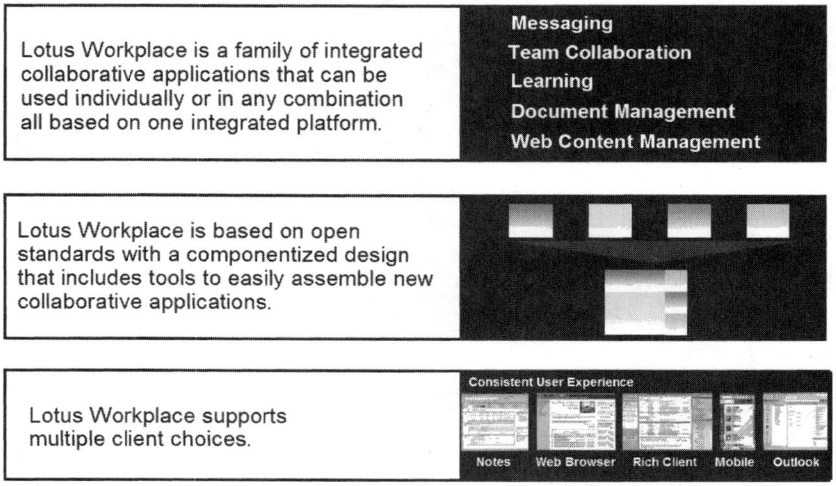

Figure 1.25. Lotus Workplace defined.

Spaces. This product helps individuals, teams, and entire organizations work together.

IBM Lotus Workplace Collaborative Learning provides learning capability that helps organizations manage their training programs more efficiently and deliver a variety of learning experiences to users.

IBM Lotus Workplace Documents provides a low-cost, standards-based collaborative document management environment with a choice of rich client or browser-based experience. This enables the management of the complete lifecycle of office documents, from collaborative authoring to review, approval, and archival. Utilizing the rich client capabilities, users can take documents offline from the server repository and edit them with their choice of office editors. They could use a locally installed set of office editor products, such as Microsoft Office, or use the built-in spreadsheet, word processing, and presentation editors, which are compatible with Microsoft Office.

As illustrated in Figure 1.26, Lotus Workplace brings together all the applications and awareness necessary for the end user; it leverages the back-end services and presents to the user the visual components that access the application function. The awareness capability of LWP can be made available throughout the user experience. Any LWP application module, such as messaging, learning, or Web conferencing can easily be integrated in a customized user view, centrally managed from the server. If Domino applications are being le-

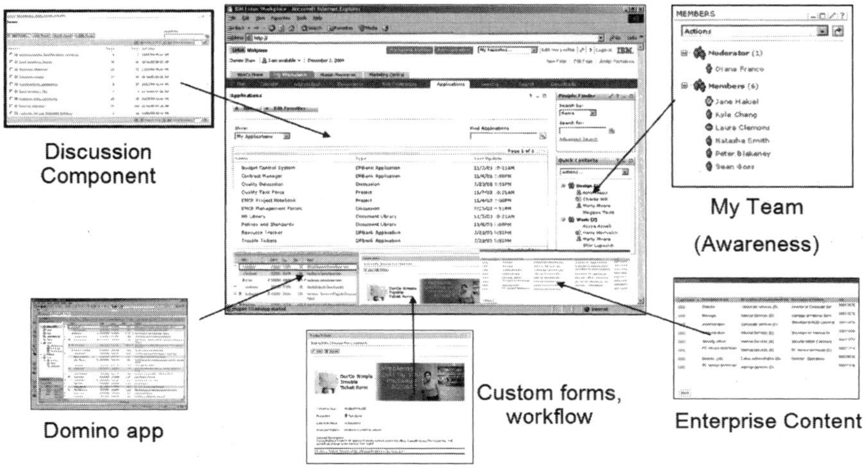

Figure 1.26. Lotus Workplace brings together applications in a shared space.

veraged via a Domino being the back-end collaboration services engine, these can be presented and integrated as appropriate to the end user, who may also be using other Lotus Workplace applications.

WebSphere Everyplace

The WebSphere Everyplace family of software enables people to have access on demand to information from a choice of devices anywhere, anytime. Everyplace software makes it possible to access data from a broad range of mobile devices. As illustrated in Figure 1.27, it delivers Web pages and business applications to the screens of cell phones and wireless mobile devices. It provides developers and service providers with tools for creating new conveniences for their customers and mobile workers.

WebSphere Everyplace Access (WEA) is also built on the WebSphere Portal infrastructure, as is Lotus Workplace. WebSphere Everyplace utilizes the WebSphere Portal services to provide the multiple client recognition that it requires to direct the right markup to the device. Portlets can be built using the same model as for WebSphere Portal, but can be enhanced to render properly on mobile devices. This allows the developer to utilize his or her Java skills to

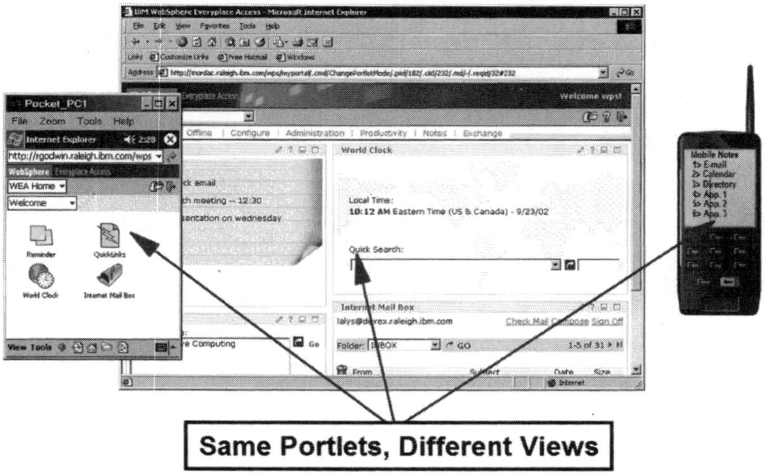

Figure 1.27. WebSphere Everyplace Access.

build mobile-based applications. This is another example of how WebSphere Portal is a key component in the IBM Workplace strategy.

WebSphere Everyplace provides an integrated client/server environment and tools for building, deploying, and managing solutions. It provides functions and services in a single Java-based middleware infrastructure with a flexibility of deployment and device choice, including cell phones, smart phones, Palm, Symbian, Research In Motion (RIM), Windows Mobile 2003, and embedded Linux operating systems. WebSphere Everyplace supports both connected and disconnected operations for real-time and intermittent access to enterprise back-end applications. It delivers the technology needed to give mobile employees access to productivity data and enterprise applications from virtually anywhere, at any time. It gives mobile employees access to productivity data and enterprise applications from pervasive devices, such as PDAs and smart phones, all from a single platform.

WebSphere Everyplace is a platform for mobile applications that includes server-side and client-side software (Everyplace Client). It provides PIM and e-mail for Lotus Notes and Microsoft Exchange PDA clients. It has all of the components required to give mobile employees access to business processes and back-office data. It is a reliable, scalable infrastructure, based on open standards, that easily integrates into an existing IT infrastructure. The proven technologies of WebSphere Application Server and WebSphere Portal Server are used to enable functions that let application developers and IBM Business Partners develop new applications and extend existing ones to mobile devices. There is an application development toolkit that includes samples, a set of plug-ins, and extensive support for portlets.

Features include high performance for e-mail/PIM synchronization, including synchronization with Microsoft Exchange servers and Lotus Domino servers, Lotus Sametime mobile support for messaging and awareness on Everyplace Client-supported Pocket PC 2002 and Palm devices.

Also included are location-aware services that easily add maps and driving directions to mobile-enabled applications, e-mail and PIM synchronization support for selected devices from NTT DoCoMo, support for additional Palm devices, and support for WebSphere Portal. Location-aware services provide a framework to integrate real-time location information in a number of business applications. For example, enterprises can provide field agents with driving directions, or locate personnel or assets. With device management functionality, system administrators can deliver critical software and security patches to remote devices, and maintain their currency. WebSphere Everyplace provides a set of tools for developing mobile solutions and for integrating them with back-end applications such as order entry, field service, repair, inventory, insurance claims processing, and supply chain systems.

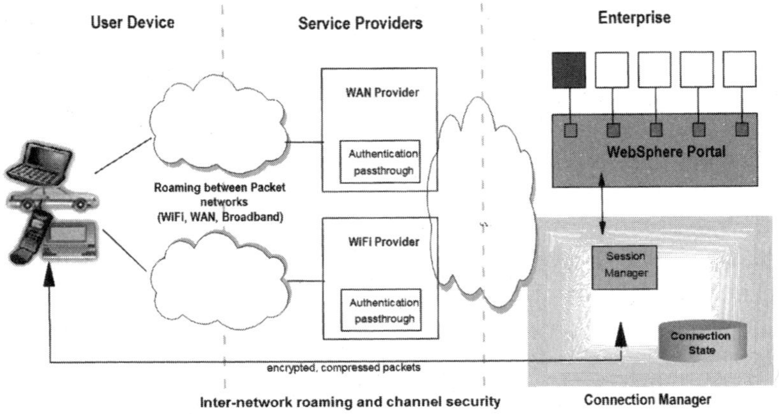

Figure 1.28. WebSphere Everyplace Connection Manager.

As illustrated in Figure 1.28, WebSphere Everyplace Connection Manager allows an enterprise to extend its existing applications to mobile workers in a cost-effective way. Connection Manager can help boost the productivity of mobile workers by giving them highly secure, uninterrupted access to the data they need. It offers a distributed, scalable, multipurpose communications platform that can help enterprises optimize bandwidth, reduce costs, and ensure security by efficiently extending their existing applications to workers in the field over many different wireless and wireline networks.

WebSphere Everyplace Connection Manager provides compression and other network optimizations that increase user response time and lower network costs; it features seamless cross-network roaming, making it possible to dynamically switch network connections without interrupting applications; it encrypts data over vulnerable wireless LAN and wireless WAN connections; and it integrates standard Internet protocols and non-IP wireless bearer networks, server hardware, device operating systems, and mobile-security protocols.

IBM Workplace Positioning

Lotus Notes/Domino versus Lotus Workplace

Many people have noticed the overlap in function between the Lotus Workplace family of products and the Lotus Notes/Domino family of products, especially with the Domino integration into WebSphere portal. Both provide browser-based collaborative services as well as a rich client. Many users not only benefit, but also require the functions provided by Notes/Domino (for example, rich mail client, group calendar scheduling, etc.). However, there are many nontraditional users who don't necessarily need all that function (such as a teacher or shop floor worker who only needs to use some corporate applications, check e-mail, or receive an electronic pay stub), for which the cost of deploying a Notes/Domino solution is harder to justify. The Lotus Workplace environment allows a business or organization to deliver the appropriate services to nontraditional users cost effectively.

Lotus Workplace is about coexistence and integration, not migration! The IBM Workplace strategy allows an organization to segment its users accordingly and provide the most cost-appropriate solution to the mix of users that exists within the organization, while ensuring that all the users can still work in an integrated environment and can collaborate. For example, the mail messaging application in Lotus Notes/Domino and the mail messaging application in Lotus Workplace both support things like SMTP (Simple Mail Transfer Protocol) and iCal is an open standard file format for calendar notices), which allows these two systems to exchange mail and calendar information easily.

Both Lotus Workplace and Notes/Domino can participate together in instant messaging and awareness, because Lotus Workplace has native support for SIP (Session-Initiated Protocol) and SIMPLE (Session-Initiated Protocol for Instant Messaging and Presence Leveraging Extensions) and Domino has SIP gateway support. The integration of these two product families will continue into the future. As illustrated in Figure 1.29, a future release of the Lotus Workplace Rich Client is expected to include the Notes client functionality, allowing the seamless integration, at the user interface, of existing Domino applications and new Lotus Workplace applications.

WebSphere Portal versus Lotus Workplace

To summarize the high level positioning of WebSphere Portal and Lotus Workplace, WebSphere Portal is about providing personalized content and access to applications to an individual. Since Lotus Workplace is built on the foundation of WebSphere Portal, it includes the WebSphere Portal capabilities, but also extends them to support the concept of teams and members in a collaborative environment. Simply put, WebSphere Portal is about "me" and Lotus Workplace is about "us."

To provide the infrastructure to support this teaming support, IBM added a significant set of collaborative services. For example, now end users are allowed to create member groups from anywhere they want and manage them.

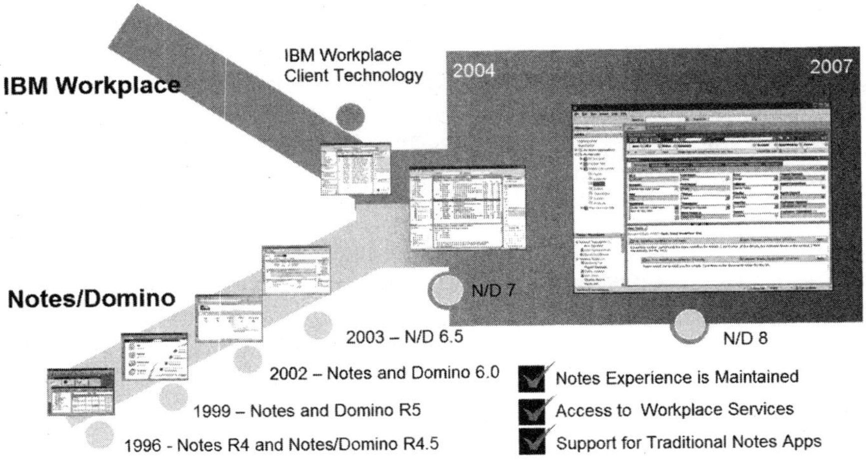

Figure 1.29. Notes/Domino and IBM Workplace roadmap.

All the services that you see—the inbox, the calendar, the awareness, the instant messaging, the Web conference, the security, and team membership—are built on top of a J2EE infrastructure. Lotus Workplaces provides one infrastructure for both the transactional side of applications as well as the collaborative side of applications. Everything is a component.

WebSphere Everyplace Access versus Lotus Workplace Mobile Support

WebSphere Everyplace can be contrasted with the mobile support in Lotus Workplace. WebSphere Everyplace provides mobile support to mobile devices (for example, PDAs and mobile phones) as an extension of the WebSphere Portal by adding synchronization services for PIM and e-mail to a variety of messaging servers, such as Domino and Microsoft Exchange. In Lotus Workplace, the mobile support has been designed as part of the server and provides a rich PDA client capability for synchronization of e-mail and document services. This is specifically designed for the Lotus Workplace server and is based on the IBM Workplace Client, Micro Edition.

2

IBM Workplace Implementation Model

Basically, what IBM has done by naming the IBM Workplace (IWP) strategy, is branded an approach to the front-end integration requirements of an overall software infrastructure. The actual four named families of products in the initial IWP announcement (WebSphere Portal, Notes/Domino, WebSphere Everyplace, and Lotus Workplace) are products that have varying degrees of adoption of the IWP technologies, principles, and standards. These product families do not actually define what IBM Workplace is, but rather are implementations of the IWP approach.

Keep in mind that, as discussed in Chapter 1, the IBM software strategy is focused on building components. It is easy to confuse product packaging versus components. Although the IWP technologies are delivered through packaged products, it's important to remember the component architecture allows for various ways of delivering the components based on changing requirements. Often a product packaging is a statement in time, and when considering the true value of the IWP model from an architectural perspective, one should think about the components, not the products. At the point of initial IWP announcement, the four families of products were the initial delivery mechanism.

In the case of WebSphere Portal, it is important to understand that WebSphere Portal should not be considered as just an application. More importantly, it provides a key part of an on demand software user interface infrastructure. Within the IWP model, WebSphere Portal services provide the mechanism for defining the user interface of applications implemented within an IWP environment.

WebSphere Everyplace implements the IWP principles of extending the user interface support of applications to mobile devices utilizing the IBM Workplace Client, Micro Edition technology.

Notes/Domino conforms to IWP strategy in the fact that it is a server-managed client environment, especially now with the "smart update" feature. Domino is an essential component of a software infrastructure, especially for collaboration services, corporate e-mail, and other aspects for which Notes/Domino products are well known. Domino also supports and integrates very nicely within an IWP implementation. Domino has powerful support for a Service Oriented Architecture and enables any Domino application to be a services-based application. As discussed in Chapter 1, it is expected that Notes Version 7 will integrate into the IWP rich client technology platform. It is also expected that with the planned Notes Version 8, the Notes client would actually be delivered as an IWP rich client, fully supporting Notes/Domino-based applications.

Lotus Workplace fully implements the IBM Workplace technologies, strategy, and principles. Because of this, Lotus Workplace is a good illustration of what the IBM Workplace strategy is all about and gives early indications of future possibilities.

IBM Workplace is a family of products and technologies that help deliver server-managed clients of choice. It supports multiple user types and end-user experiences, across a wide range of access points and forms of connectivity, thus enabling flexible and cost-effective collaborative access for people, business processes, applications, and content. As illustrated in Figure 2.1, IBM Workplace provides the front-end integration of the total application infrastructure. IBM Workplace is about the part of the portfolio that people use to interact with business.

IBM Workplace is a "game changer" which many companies are embracing and have been working with IBM as early adopters of this model.

With the IBM Workplace architecture, IBM has provided the power of one architectural model, one programming model, one consistent tool—and all of it standards based. This enables flexible and cost-effective access to people, business processes, applications, and content.

Back-End Integration Model

Understanding the back-end integration model is important, as it is key part of the IBM Workplace model. Below is a brief discussion of the back-end integration model. For a detailed explanation of this part of the model, please refer to

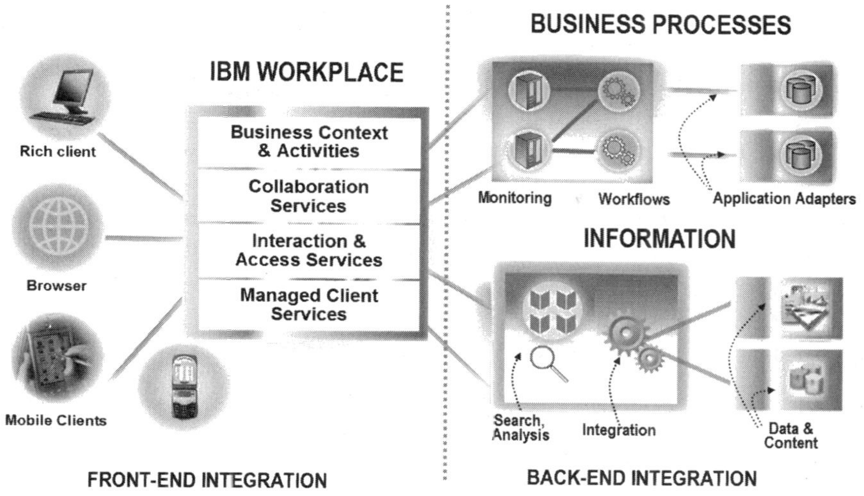

Figure 2.1. IBM Workplace, enabling server managed clients.

the book *IBM Software for e-business on demand* by Douglas W. Spencer (co-author of this book).

Business Processes

Business process back-end services provide the necessary integration and capability for managing business processes that may involve a diversity of internal and external systems, human participation, and rules that need to be enforced. These are often the most complex of issues for IT executives to facilitate. As businesses' imperatives change, IT systems and processes need to respond. To quickly achieve business objectives and improve business performance, companies need to evolve from manual business processes to automated ones. To provide higher levels of service to users, companies need unprecedented levels of integration to link legacy systems, such as customer relationship management, enterprise resource planning, supply-chain management, and other intra-enterprise systems. This can be accomplished through modeling, automating, and combining current and new processes within a company and across the value chain of partners and customers.

Information

Information back-end software provides the information infrastructure for integrating vast amounts of heterogeneous information from a variety of sources. Information integration software links the diverse sources of information as if they formed a single database. Business intelligence software senses and identifies trends in data, in real time, for decision making. Content management software helps manage digital media and information assets, allowing users to quickly retrieve information records in the context needed. Data management tools reduce the complexity of managing database systems and aim to achieve better system utilization with less operator skill and fewer resources.

Web Services

Web Services is a collection of standards that enable the dynamic discovery and integration of applications as part of an on demand business model. The largest jump in productivity acceleration usually occurs when a mix of parallel technologies mature and converge, and awareness and adoption of these technologies increases to a mass scale, which makes it worthwhile for other activities to happen: this is the "magic" that will cause a huge jump in productivity. We use the word *magic* because some of the "other activities" happen without people realizing it until after the fact. Of course, then it's too late for some organizations to capture the first-to-adopt advantage. Nonetheless, the magic happens. The rate of adoption of Web Services is difficult to predict precisely, but we do know about many organizations and businesses that are doing a lot of work implementing Web Services, and the momentum is definitely growing.

Dynamic business is about the automation of applications, discovering other applications, using standards for determining how to connect together, and what format of information can be exchanged. Web Services enables business on demand in order to leverage internal or external resources. The Internet, industry standards, the adoption of Web application standards, the proliferation of implemented Web applications across the globe in all industries, the awareness and utilization of Web-based applications by people on a mass scale, and so on have all converged to enable on demand businesses.

Within a computer or computer system could be applications that leverage the services of other applications. Web Services is cost-effective, reliable, secure, embraced by many vendors, and enabled by industry standards. There are many solutions that make implementing Web Services relatively easy.

Simply put, Web Services enables applications to interact with each other using Web standards. The architecture for Web Services is based on open Internet standards for description, discovery, and invocation. These services or applications can be published and discovered dynamically. They can be platform and implementation neutral. For example, Microsoft .Net applications can integrate, using Web Services, with IBM WebSphere (Java-based) applications.

The requirements of Web Services are facilitated by standards. For example, the need to communicate between applications can be facilitated using XML messaging. Simple Object Access Protocol (SOAP) can be used to invoke functions on remote systems to perform given operations (a request message is sent by service requester; a response message may be sent by service provider; the message may be asynchronous). The need to describe services can be facilitated by the service specification language, which is the Web Services Description Language (WSDL), which is an implementation of XML.

Web Services incorporates a mix of emerging standards that are supported by a variety of vendors. There is significant industry support from IBM, Microsoft, BEA, Sun, Oracle, and other companies. Web Services Interoperability (WS-I) is an organization founded by IBM and Microsoft to achieve seamless interoperability across Web Services implementations from different vendors. WS-Security is a standards process to define message-level security for SOAP. This is in the early stages of definition, and there are competing proposals from several of the vendors. WS-BPEL (Business Process Execution Language for Web Services) is a standard for the specification on how to describe workflow processes within Web Services.

Service Oriented Architecture

Businesses want to integrate existing systems and support business processes that span the entire business value chain. A mix of designs are used, ranging from rigid point-to-point interactions to Web actions. By using the Internet, IT systems are made available internally and externally, but the interactions are not flexible and are without a standardized architecture.

Figure 2.2 illustrates an Enterprise Service Bus, which enables a Services Oriented Architecture (SOA). SOA is about applications being provided as a collection of services that communicate with each other. The Enterprise Service Bus enables the passing of data from one service to another and coordinates activities between services.

Because of this increasing demand for technologies that support connecting and sharing of resources and data, there is a need for a flexible, standardized

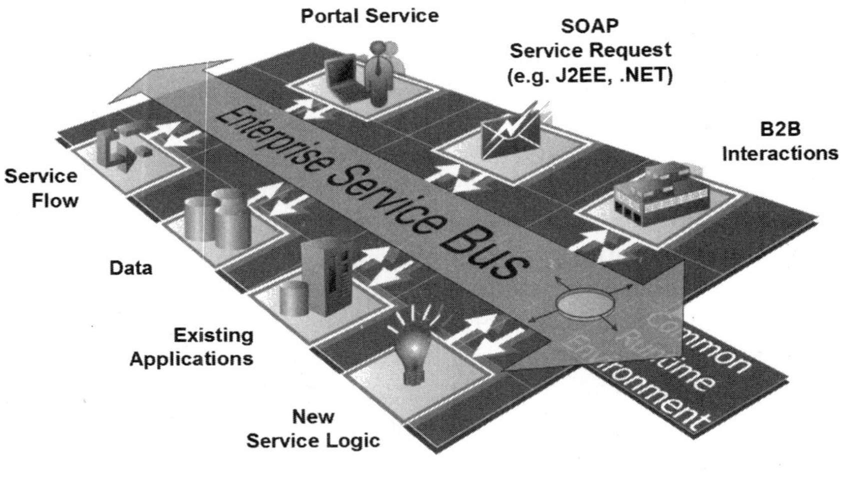

Figure 2.2. Service Oriented Architecture enabled by an Enterprise Service Bus.

architecture. Service Oriented Architecture (SOA) is a flexible architecture that unifies business processes by structuring large applications into building blocks (small modular functional units or services) to be used by different groups of people within and outside a company. The building blocks can fill one of three roles: service provider, service broker, or service requester.

Service Provider

The service provider creates a Web service and possibly publishes its interface and access information to the service registry. Each provider must decide which services to expose; how to make trade-offs between security and easy availability; how to price the services; or, if they are free, how to exploit them for other value. The provider also has to decide the category in which the service should be listed for a given broker service and what sort of trading partner agreements are required to use the service.

Service Broker

The service broker, also known as a *service registry*, is responsible for making the Web service interface and implementation access information available to any potential service requestor. The implementer of the broker decides about the scope of the broker. Public brokers are available through the Internet, whereas private brokers are accessible only to a limited audience (for example, users of a company intranet). Furthermore, the amount of information offered has to be decided. Some brokers specialize in many listings. Others offer high levels of trust in the listed services. Some cover a broad landscape of services, and others focus within an industry. There are also brokers that catalogue other brokers. Depending on the business model, brokers can attempt to maximize look-up requests, number of listings, or accuracy of the listings.

Service Requestor

The service requestor or Web service client locates entries in the broker registry using various find operations and then binds to the service provider in order to invoke one of its Web Services. To use an SOA efficiently requires interoperability between different systems and programming languages, clear and unambiguous description language for the syntax of the service interface, and a search mechanism to retrieve suitable services.

Why Do We Need a Service Oriented Architecture?

Service Oriented Architecture enables distributed computing, treating software resources like services available on a network. The power and flexibility that SOAs potentially offer the enterprise are substantial. If an organization abstracts its IT infrastructure so that it presents its functionality in the form of coarse-grained services that offer clear business value, then the consumers of those services (whether they are at the same company or at one of that company's business partners) can access them independently of the underlying technology that supports them. Furthermore, if service consumers can discover and bind to available services while they are active, then the IT infrastructure behind those services can offer extraordinary flexibility to the businesses that invoke them.

Web Services is well suited to enable an SOA in which the solutions consist of collections of autonomous services that use Web Services standards to integrate. Web Services provides for interoperability between software components that can communicate between different companies and can reside on different infrastructures. This basic set of Web-service specifications allows businesses and software vendors to solve important problems. Service Oriented Architecture is a natural complement to the object-oriented, procedural, and data-centric approaches to solution implementations. This is opening new possibilities in distributed application development.

The Web Services approach to a Service Oriented Architecture is to make functional building blocks accessible over standard Internet protocols that are independent from platforms and programming languages. These services can be new applications or wrapped around existing legacy systems to make them network enabled. A service can rely on another service to achieve its goals.

WebSphere Application Server provides an application integration bus that is standards based, combines synchronous and asynchronous communications, enables dynamic business integration, is secure and flexible, and has tools to help simplify the development of SOA application environments. WebSphere Application provides this Enterprise Service Bus infrastructure that enables a highly scalable and efficient model for implementing SOA. WebSphere is a core underlying component within the IWP architecture, thus enabling the IWP environment for SOA.

IBM Workplace Embraces Service Oriented Architecture

The IWP approach is one that fully embraces Service Oriented Architecture (SOA) and the standards of Web Services. Service Oriented Architectures allow reuse of applications and data by rendering software components as services, thereby speeding project deployments and application changes. Many vendors are heavily promoting the SOA model. This is encouraging many smaller, niche IT vendors to form alliances to provide companies with ranges of SOA components and subsystems made from parts that are proven to work together. Part of the objective of SOAs is to enable different applications and technologies to interact. IBM Workplace also provides a range of components that businesses and business partners can leverage and build other components that will work well together.

IBM Workplace Implementation Model

Figure 2.3 illustrates the high-level architectural view of the IWP implementation model. Application services from the back end are delivered through a portal infrastructure to various types of managed clients. Remembering that IWP supports browser-based, rich client-based, and mobile-based client envi-

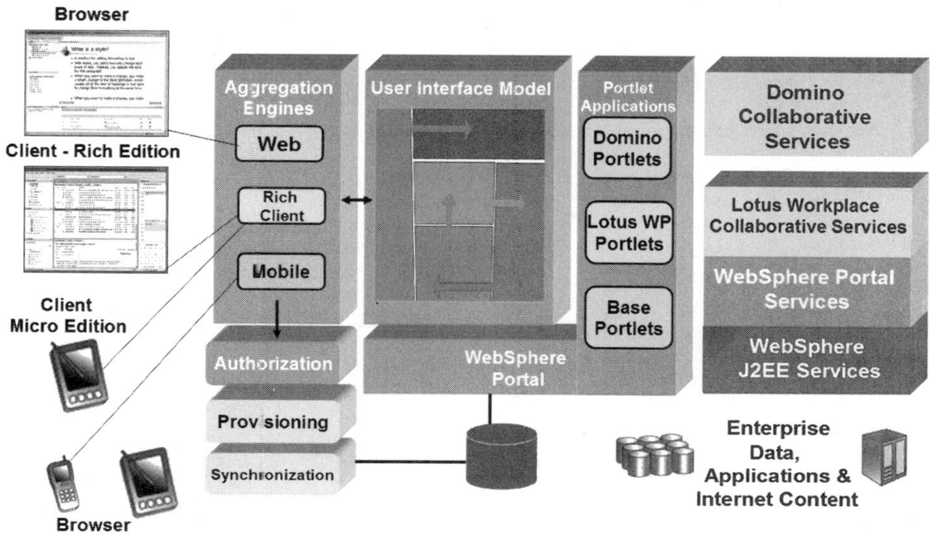

Figure 2.3. IBM Workplace implementation model.

ronments, the IWP provides corresponding aggregation engines that render the application appropriately to the end user.

Positioning IWP versus Microsoft's Approach

As you can see, the portal infrastructure is absolutely fundamental to the delivery of applications in the IWP model. This approach is a key differentiator compared with other vendor rich client implementations. For example, Microsoft's well publicized "Longhorn" strategy does not leverage Microsoft's existing portal infrastructure, putting into question the future viability of their current portal product. Architecturally, IBM has adopted the IWP approach, which is based on open standards and therefore can be implemented in a variety of operating environments. Additionally, IBM is building on the substantial market acceptance of the portal approach and extends that now to multiple clients, not just the browser. Therefore, the IWP approach is protecting the investment companies make today in implementing their current On Demand Business requirements, while laying the foundation for future requirements.

WebSphere Portal

The WebSphere Portal architecture is more than just a Web aggregation engine, it actually enables a well-conceived infrastructure with a complete set of capabilities that can be used to write applications. The API (application programming interface) piece of the WebSphere Portal is a key piece of portal infrastructure. The API provides support for one of the standards that is part of the larger Java standards environment called *JSR168,* and it supports the portlet API. This is an extension of what has been in Java for many years and called *servlets* and *JSPs* (Java Server Pages).

Servlets and JSPs were designed around the idea that when you wrote that type of code, whatever you were sending to a browser it owned the browser window. With a portlet you can do everything that you can do with a servlet with the idea that the portlet doesn't own the whole browser because there is going to be a window manager controlling where it got placed inside the browser. Portlets are first-class Java applications.

In order to really have a portal server that does more than just give you the ability to write applications, there are many services that the portal must provide to ensure the security and reliability of such. For example, WebSphere Portal provides authentication services to make sure people are authenticated with the portal and get access to all the different resources. This service is also available as an API to any portlet.

Figure 2.4 shows some of the many services that portlet writers have access to, such as Globalization. Globalization allows you to write a portlet with which you can ask the server what language the user is coming in as, either on the browser or through preferences, and then you can send to the user the appropriate translated information. Device management allows for different device types and markups to be recognized by the portal so the appropriate date formats can be sent. All of the administration of the portal is done with portlets. There is not a separate administration system. Search and document management are also base functions of the portal.

Let's look at some of the key services. Customizing of the portal is a very important service. This is done through a service called *Themes and Skins*, which are based on standard cascading style sheets and HTML that a Web page designer could create. The look of the portal is completely controlled

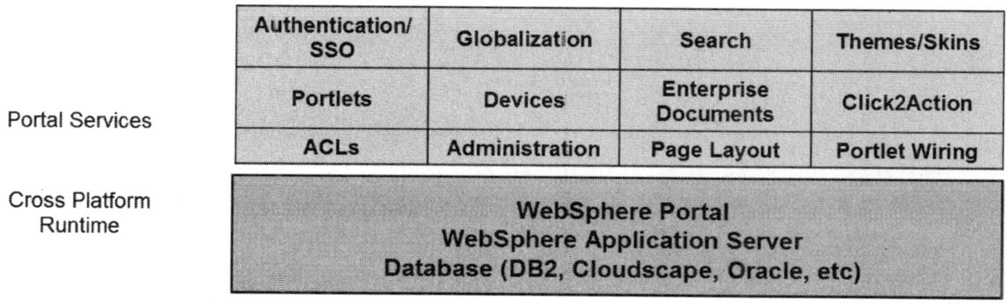

Figure 2.4. WebSphere Portal services.

though these themes and it is even changeable based on user roles. Certain people or groups can have a different look and feel than others. Users can create personal pages if allowed, and administrators can set different areas of the page they can lock down. For example, at the corporate level, you can configure the page to lock down important portlets that you want to make sure are included in all divisions of your company, such as the corporate news. However, you can delegate the rest of the portal page to the content owners in each division, allowing them to update that piece of the portal with their content but they cannot delete the corporate content. In fact, you can delegate right down to the end user so that he or she can put anything they have access to in that space. This allows you to provide an automatic governance system within the infrastructure

Once portlets are in place on the page, you can now start to create interactions between them. A standards-based approach was built that allows portlets to talk to each other even though they might have been developed by different people at different times. This is done through a Web Services infrastructure. Every portlet inside the WebSphere Portal server is by default a Web service. When a portlet is instantiated on a page, the portal server knows how to communicate with it because a Web Services Description Language (WSDL) document is associated with it. The portal server will see whether there are any matching inputs and outputs automatically. If there are some, then the portal will actually create menus to allow the user to move data between them. Taking that to the next level, you can start to wire applications together. For example, two portlets written by two people at different times can be made to appear as a single application. You start to assemble applications inside the portal environment. This capability is called *Click2Action* and *Portlet Wiring*.

There is the capability for easily creating portlets through the WebSphere Portal Application Integrator (WPAI). These are portlet factories that allow you to build portlets to connect to a wide variety of back-end systems. For example there are builders for SAP, PeopleSoft, Siebel, Domino, and relational databases. They take advantage of the portal infrastructure to allow communications between them. You could take a PeopleSoft portlet and directly hook it up to a Domino application with no coding.

As illustrated in Figure 2.5, for the delivery of applications to the user, WebSphere Portal has been designed to manage the user interface model. The description of what a user sees is defined within the portal infrastructure as a data model along with the interactions between the components in that user interface. In the simplest form, a browser receives a request to display an application and the aggregation engine determines which authority the user has to determine what the user is allowed to see. The aggregation engine then looks at the data in the user interface model and renders the appropriate HTML to the browser.

This model provides for a flexible environment where browser-based applications can be easily customized and personalized by manipulating the user interface model definition. Building a powerful Web application becomes a simplified administration task instead of a complicated programming task.

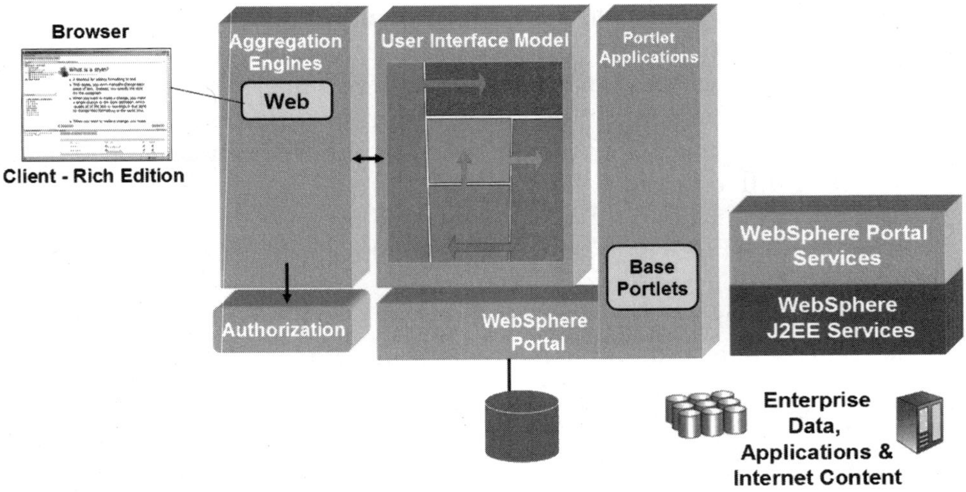

Figure 2.5. IBM Workplace implementation model with WebSphere Portal.

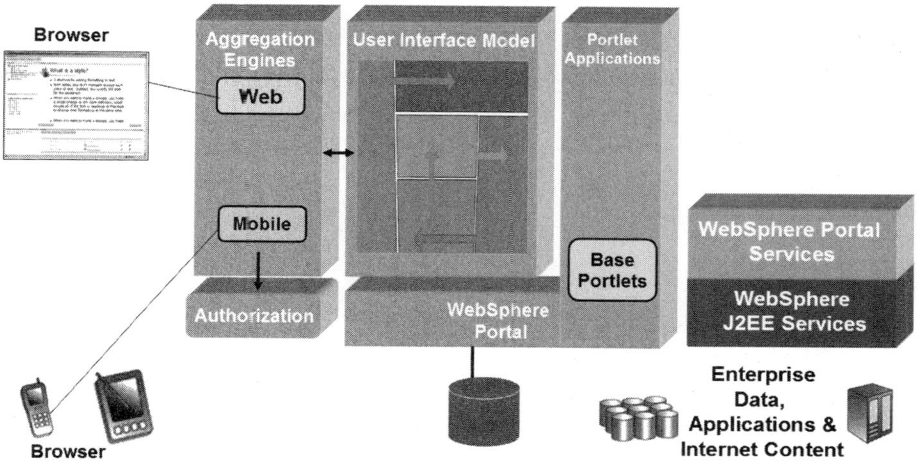

Figure 2.6. IBM Workplace implementation model with WebSphere Everyplace Access.

WebSphere Everyplace Access

With the addition of WebSphere Everyplace Access (WEA) into the IWP infrastructure (see Figure 2.6), an additional aggregation engine gets added to the environment. A key feature of WebSphere Portal is its ability to recognize the various types of client devices that can make requests (for example, browsers, different PDAs, cell phones). Each of these clients provides a unique identifier, which the aggregation engine can be customized to recognize. This capability of the portal provides a flexible approach to define today's and tomorrow's clients. With the WEA addition, when a PDA or cell phone makes a request to the portal, the aggregation engine still determines the authorization and looks at the same user interface data model, but now recognizing that it is not an HTML device, it can build the appropriate mark-up language information for that device (for example, WML).

Lotus Domino

As illustrated in Figure 2.7, and discussed in this chapter, Domino plays an important part in this IWP infrastructure model by providing the ability to

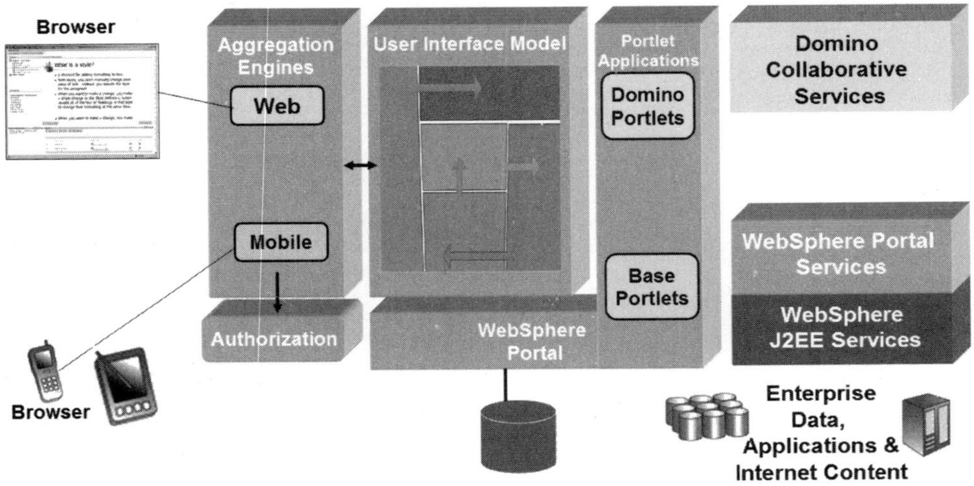

Figure 2.7. IBM Workplace implementation model with Lotus Domino.

build a dynamic collaborative workplace by leveraging Domino-based applications. There are thousands of applications that are built on Domino that are core business process applications for organizations all over the world. It is important to understand that Domino is a strategic foundational collaborative application environment that coexists and integrates with products such as WebSphere Portal and Lotus Workplace.

Lotus Domino is a comprehensive application platform (see Figure 2.8) for collaboration workflow that handles both connected and disconnected requirements for data and applications. Domino provides a complete infrastructure to create, test, deploy, and manage distributed, multilingual applications. It can facilitate a directory, data, Web applications, Java applications, administration, security, and connectivity, and be a foundation for server-based applications.

Domino is designed to empower developers and extend existing application investments. Domino supports IBM DB2 as an optional data store, enabling developers to build applications that can leverage both the Domino document-based model and the DB2 relational file model. Developers can bring SQL query capability and an entire industry of mature and proven reporting tools to use with their Domino applications.

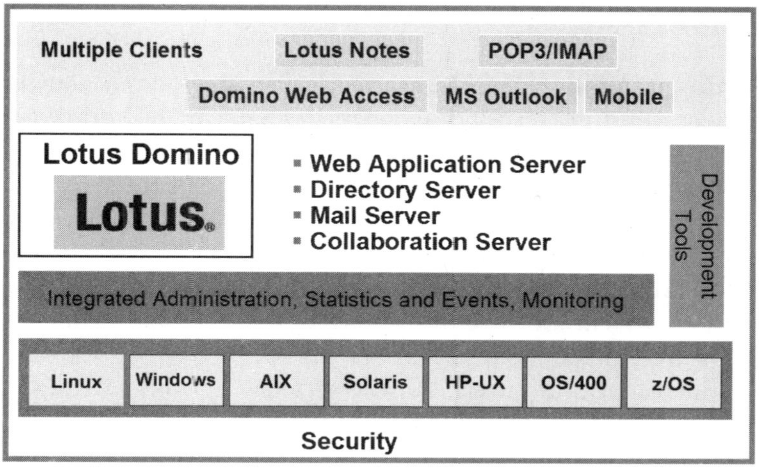

Figure 2.8. Lotus Domino application platform.

Domino has a Web Services design element that lets developers use Domino as a Web Services host, and use Java or LotusScript to surface pieces of Domino applications as Web Services. Developers can use the development skills they already have to surface their existing applications in an open Web Services implementation. Domino also gives developers more control over the way Domino applications are surfaced in WebSphere Portal. Lotus has built Domino to leverage the strengths of DB2, Web Services, J2EE, and WebSphere Portal, which will enable Notes developers not only to enrich their existing Domino application investments, but to reuse them over a much broader domain.

To provide integration with the Domino base applications, WebSphere Portal includes the portlets necessary for that integration. This includes portlets for messaging, instant messaging, team rooms, and documents so that you can provide a single integrated view. There are many different ways of connecting to Domino data within the portal. For example, there is a portlet builder that allows basic access to the Domino data. There are a number of prebuilt portlets so that you can take those functions and start to integrate them together to make the end-user experience much easier. The Domino Web Application Portlet is effectively a proxy portlet that allows a developer to grab the input stream as it is coming out of the Domino engine and remap what Domino wants to write so that everything can be kept inside the portal.

Lotus Workplace

As illustrated in Figure 2.9, Lotus Workplace provides a new set of collaborative services and corresponding portlets that can be utilized within an IWP infrastructure and provide several architectural benefits.

To summarize in a few words, portal and the portal services are about personalizing for "me" (my news, my mail, etc). Lotus Workplace is about "us." It's about working together in teams. To provide the infrastructure to support this, IBM added a new layer of services to run on top of the portal. For example, now we can allow end users to create member groups from anywhere they want and allow them to manage it.

As illustrated in Figure 2.10, the services (inbox, calendar, awareness, instant messaging, Web conference, security, team membership, etc.) are built on top of a J2EE and portal infrastructure. This provides one infrastructure for both the transactional side of your applications as well as the collaborative side of your applications. Everything is component based. When IBM built the calendar for Web conferencing scheduling, and built the calendar for the personal calendar, they look the same because they are using the same component. These components are Web Services within the infrastructure of Workplace. That allows for a mixing and matching of the components the way

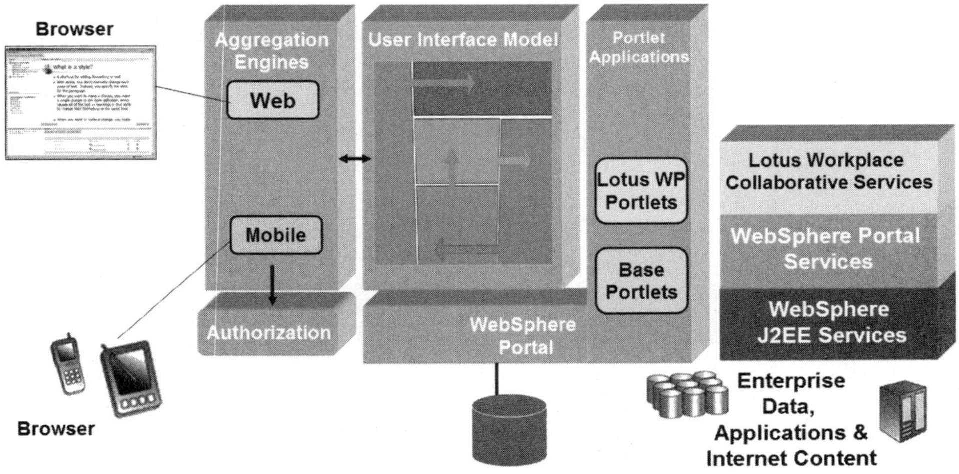

Figure 2.9. IBM Workplace implementation model with Lotus Workplace.

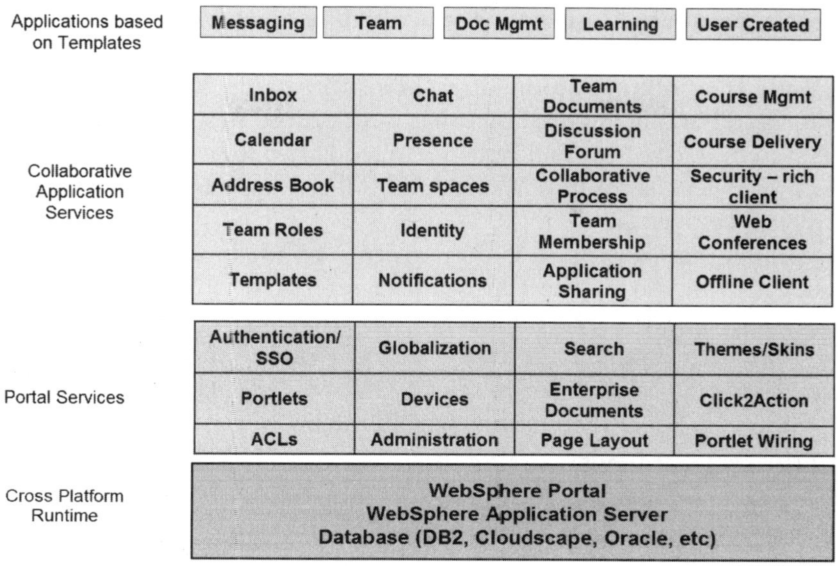

Figure 2.10. Lotus Workplace collaborative application services.

that you want to produce the applications. The top row are the applications that you can buy from IBM, such as Lotus Workplace Messaging, Lotus Workplace Team Collaboration, Lotus Workplace Document Management, and Lotus Workplace Learning.

What IBM did is piece together the components as a set of applications. These were done with a look and function built on the Lotus Workplace services components and presented as IBM and the Lotus development team decided would be a good combination and use. But, because the underlying services are components, they can be put together in different ways. This whole approach is providing for very different ways of looking at collaboration that are not following the stereotypical implementations of collaboration applications. This is another "game changing" approach that will spawn new ideas for how people collaborate and will enable new business designs. For example, for the calendar function, on top of the calendar service provided by Lotus Workplace, IBM built a calendar user interface based on portlets, etc. You could build your own interface if you wanted.

Another component is the person object. In Lotus Workplace, the person service becomes a first class object in the architecture. Wherever a person name appears within the Lotus Workplace family of products, there are actions that can be performed. For example, starting a chat if the person is online, sending an e-mail, or looking up the directory information for that person are all available via a dynamic menu. Since this is an object, new functions can be added to the system. Cisco, for example, changed this one person object to integrate its voice-over-IP system into Workplace. All the applications are now enabled for Cisco voice over IP.

Managing Workplace is done from a policy-based system. A management policy allows you to affect how a user interacts with the system. For example, in the licensing policy, you can set out what you are licensed to use. This is a trust-only environment, so if you buy any one of the products the entire infrastructure is installed and you select what you are licensed for. You can even get down to very specific functions within the products. Through user policies, you can turn on or off specific functions.

Rich Client and Micro Edition

IBM Workplace Client Technology extends the security, manageability, and component-based assembly of a server-based platform to the desktop and pervasive devices. This provides an innovative model for building rich, reusable client applications. It will be the foundation for the next-generation, rich end-user experience for both enterprises and small-to-midsize businesses. IBM Workplace embraces open standards with IBM Workplace Client Technology and provides flexible access for a complete range of user experiences—on both desktop and mobile devices—via a dynamically downloaded client platform.

There are three aspects to consider when discussing the IWP Client Technology. First, we'll discuss the specific client technology and how it is built. Second, we'll outline what server components are required to support the client and how they work. And third, we'll discuss how the client environment is managed from the server.

IBM Workplace Client Technology, Rich Client Edition

The core client technology platform is based on the Eclipse technology, which provides the Java run-time environment for general desktop applications, an application user interface, and a flexible architecture (see Figure 2.11), that is

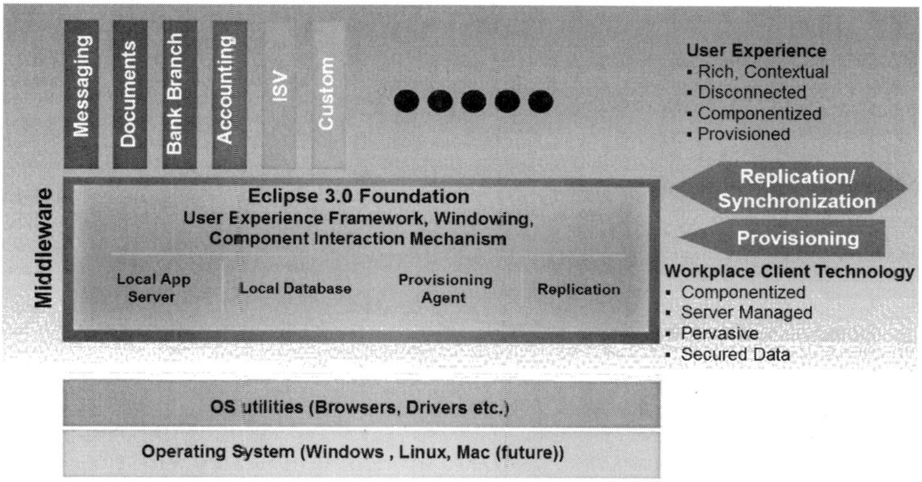

Figure 2.11. IBM Workplace Client Technology.

easily extended and supports multiple operating systems. Add-on generic contributions are being developed through a cooperative effort between IBM and the Eclipse organization.

IBM is building the Workplace Client Technology with heavy use of standards-based components. For example, in addition to the Eclipse framework, IBM is reusing the IBM Cloudscape data store (acquired when IBM acquired Informix), and an application run-time environment from the IBM WebSphere team called *IBM Extension Services for WebSphere Everyplace*. Synchronization capabilities are delivered through support of the SyncML standard that IBM is continuing to drive.

WebSphere Portal software is used as the aggregation framework. The IBM user interface layer provides reusable components, such as rich text editor, live names, and custom tables that tie into extension services and can be used in applications built either by IBM or other providers. IBM Lotus Workplace shared application components make up the Lotus Workplace collaboration platform and were used to create products such as IBM Lotus Workplace Messaging, IBM Lotus Workplace Documents, and other applications that third parties can build.

IBM Workplace Client Technology supports a variety of client operating systems, including Linux distributions; Microsoft Windows on the desktop; and, as currently planned, Macintosh OS—as well as a range of mobile devices.

IBM Workplace Client Technology provides a no-touch deployment model coupled with policy-based management to help reduce the cost of managing the end user's desktop environment. IBM Workplace Client Technology provides built-in security features, such as a local, encrypted data store that synchronizes with the server environment (to support both connected and disconnected operations), and the ability to help ensure that all applications running are provisioned and digitally signed by a trusted source.

IBM Workplace Client Server Components

As illustrated in Figure 2.12, in the server environment that supports the IWP client, there is a provisioning engine that communicates with the corresponding component in the client, a synchronization engine that responds to the SyncML requests from the client, and a rich client aggregation engine to support the new markup content required for the client. Today, these services are delivered in the Lotus Workplace product family. However, because this is a component-based model, there could be future product offerings that take advantage of this implementation.

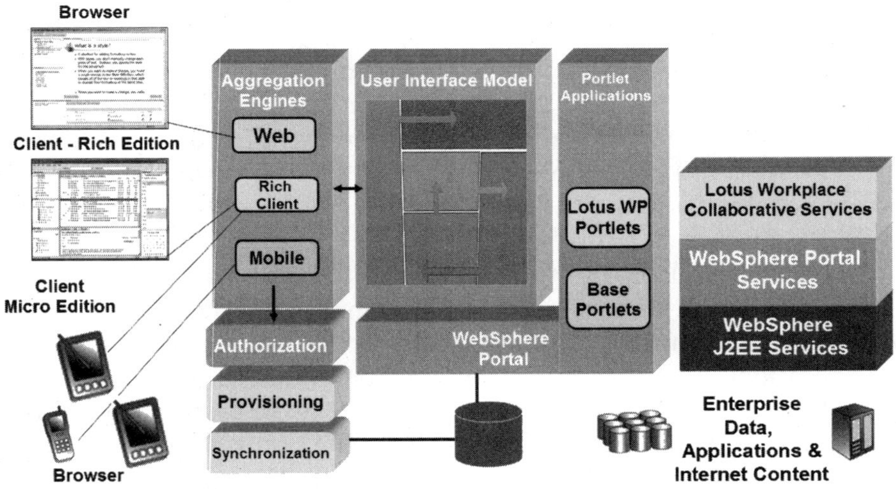

Figure 2.12. IBM Workplace implementation model with IBM Workplace Client Technology.

How IBM Workplace Platform Rich Client Works

The Workplace rich client has management characteristics of a Web application. The portal server is managing the components used in the Workplace client and also driving the aggregation of the user interface element. As illustrated in Figure 2.13, when a user logs on to the portal, a model of the user's page is created, by finding out what pages and portlets the user is authorized to see. The markup for those portlets is aggregated to make the Web page that gets delivered to the browser.

As illustrated in Figure 2.14, applying the same model to the Workplace client, when the user logs on to the portal, the same assembly process produces a model of what this user is meant to see. However, instead of assembling an HTML page, we assemble an XML stream that indicates which Eclipse plug-ins should be loaded. When this stream is received on the client side, the Workplace client framework uses the instructions to load the necessary plug-ins. If the plug-in is not already installed on the client, the provisioning agent in the client makes a request to provisioning server component to download the appropriate plug-in.

The XML stream is cached on the client so that you can work disconnected. Each client plug-in is a native Eclipse plug-in, so its rendering is truly native. To say this a different way, the XML stream is used only for provision-

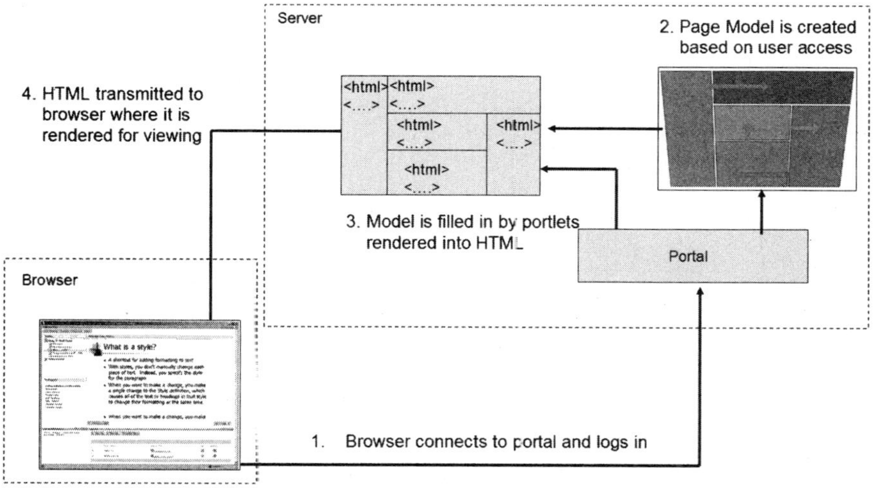

Figure 2.13. Typical browser portal flow.

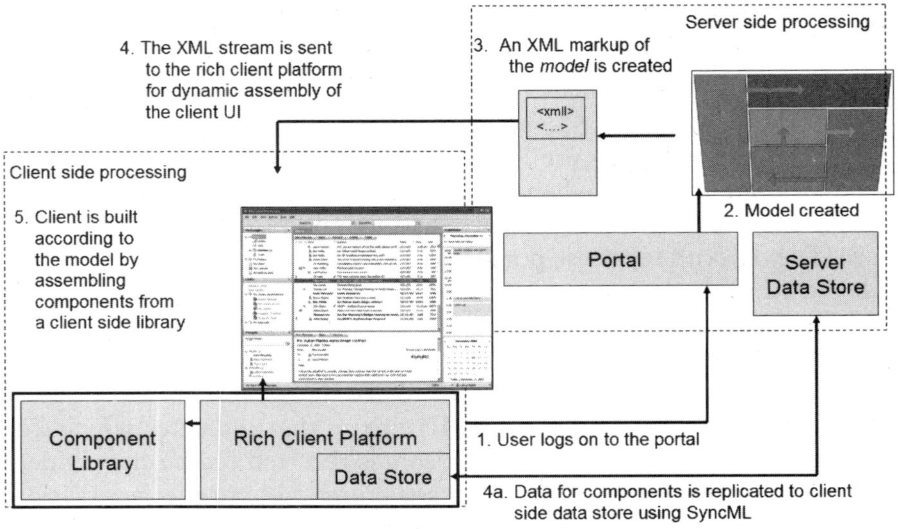

Figure 2.14. IBM Workplace Client flow.

ing the client, not for any of the rendering process. When the plug-in actually runs, they use either local or remote EJB calls to obtain the data that they need (such as calendar or mail information). Data for the business components is cached in a lightweight, local database, and is replicated to and from the server using SyncML.

IBM Workplace Client Technology, Micro Edition

Everything discussed in this chapter thus far has focused on the rich desktop user experience. But another aspect of IBM Workplace Client Technology is that the same core components that deliver a rich Managed Client model for desktop-based experiences can also be deployed within applications where a smaller footprint is required.

As illustrated in Figure 2.15, the IWP Client Technology, Micro Edition is an embedded middleware framework that enables application and services deployment, device configuration, and lifecycle management to a wide spectrum of mobile and pervasive devices via the same server-managed infrastructure

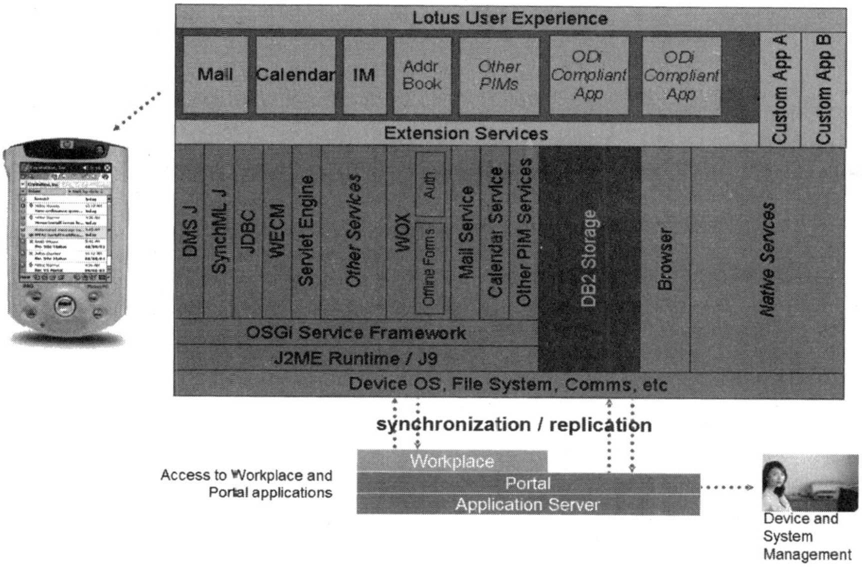

Figure 2.15. IBM Workplace Client Micro Edition.

already discussed. This product was previously called WebSphere Everyplace, Micro Edition.

The IWP Client Technology, Micro Edition is adaptable to network conditions. It can be frustrating to lose connection for voice, but for data applications it is even worse, because you end up having to start over if connection is lost. This solution addresses the need to maintain the session, even if connectivity is lost.

Device lifecycles are shorter than the application lifecycle. Businesses need a platform that extends the lifecycle of applications and allows them to live through multiple device generations, and the IWP Client Technology Platform, Micro Edition provides this capability.

3

Lotus Workplace Family

As commonly known, to best understand where we are going, we need to know where we've been. As illustrated in Figure 3.1, in the early 1980s (when Lotus was one of the first with personal productivity applications, such as spreadsheet, word processing, and presentation), the main goal was to support personal productivity. As these products matured, we found that users often needed

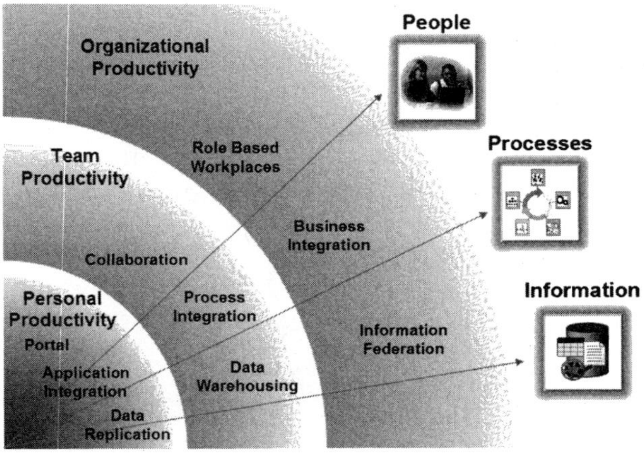

Figure 3.1. Three waves of productivity: Personal, Team, and Organizational.

the capability to work together as a team. For example, if you were editing a document, multiple people may need to be involved. Thus, we began to add function for teaming into the actual personal productivity products. Although this was good, it wasn't always the most effective way to address the need.

The era of team productivity was created when Lotus Domino and Notes came along. "Team Productivity" was the design point of this product family. E-mail became a mission-critical application and Web conferencing, discussion threads, instant messaging, awareness, and document management became widely adopted. It should be noted that this second wave of collaboration did not displace the personal productivity products but rather incorporated them into the new technologies. Today, more documents are being created in e-mail systems than in any word processing package.

As the team productivity has matured, businesses are finding the requirement to integrate these collaborative services with their traditional back-end systems. It's about getting the people, the business processes, and the information within an organization connected.

The newest wave of collaboration can be called *organizational productivity*, or *business productivity*. This area is about combining the strengths/capabilities of personal productivity and team productivity, thus enabling better business productivity. This is what the IBM Workplace products and strategy are aimed at addressing.

At organizations of all sizes, IT executives like the power and flexibility of the Notes/Domino environment for collaboration. But now they also want more. They want the function of such a powerful collaboration system to be enabled in a standards-based environment. They want the functions componentized, so they can mix and match modules as needed. They want to have the collaborative services components moved up to "enterprise class" to ensure a higher level of support, reliability, and extensibility across the enterprise. Instead of creating a user interface where a user has to go to an e-mail system to access mail, then go to a document repository to access documents, then go to another user interface for instant messaging or team rooms, they want one dynamic environment that brings all of these together efficiently.

IBM Lotus Workplace

The IBM Lotus Workplace family provides an innovative environment for collaboration and human interaction that uses a single, open platform to integrate people with business processes.

Lotus Workplace provides collaborative products that can be experienced through a choice of security-rich clients, such as a browser, desktop systems, or mobile devices. This family of products gives people simplified access and interaction with other people and a host of collaborative capabilities such as e-mail, calendaring and scheduling, instant messaging, Web conferencing, Team Spaces, document and Web content management, and learning. Also included with Lotus Workplace is a set of tools to easily create a new workplace that can be applied to fit specific industry or business needs.

As the industry addresses the next wave of business productivity requirements, the Lotus Workplace family will enable a necessary common user interface that makes it easier for people to communicate and collaborate with others, both internally and externally, and enables users to work together to respond more quickly and accurately, reducing redundancies, and driving simplification into business processes. Thinking beyond the traditional office productivity applications, while also incorporating such functions as needed, the business requirements will evolve, and, as more people utilize the Lotus Workplace family, they will discover new ways of doing things.

Lotus Workplace is capable of delivering a variety of server-managed client experiences, ranging from browser-based to a new, full rich client. The server-managed client model provides administrators a secure, no-touch deployment model coupled with central policy-based management of the end user's desktop environment. This simplifies IT operational support by providing a common infrastructure to manage and deploy while reducing costs.

IBM has created a path for organizations to be able to leverage existing software assets such as Lotus Notes and Domino or WebSphere Portal and still take advantage of the capabilities in the Lotus Workplace collaboration platform. With new products and enhancements made to existing Lotus Workplace products, IBM supports the future growth plan for all of its current customers, whether Lotus Notes and Domino-based or portal-based. In addition, these products can benefit current J2EE-based organizations and how these open-standards products can be integrated with infrastructure and application investments from other vendors. Organizations can continue to use current and future releases of Lotus Notes and Domino, and other Lotus software products, as they can be integrated into the Lotus Workplace environment using new portlets and tools. They can purchase and implement IBM WebSphere Portal to extend the reach of current investments.

The core family of Lotus Workplace products include Lotus Workplace Messaging, Lotus Workplace Team Collaboration, Lotus Workplace Documents, Lotus Workplace Collaborative Learning, and Lotus Workplace Builder.

Lotus Workplace Messaging

Lotus Workplace Messaging (see Figure 3.2) provides just the right level of messaging functionality to address the range of needs for all employees (traditional and nontraditional), such as an e-mail inbox, address book, and folders. These functions are provided in an intuitive browser-based interface, making it very cost effective to deliver.

Lotus Workplace Messaging delivers a cost-efficient messaging solution that allows organizations to easily extend enterprise e-mail to users currently without a dedicated workspace or e-mail access. This provides an easy-to-use, industrial-strength, Web-based messaging solution to deskless workers that includes e-mail, a personal calendar, and a personal address book. It eliminates the need to manage, update, and support complex desktop-client software.

This can also be deployed with other Lotus Workplace products to utilize the added benefits of a unified collaborative work environment. Most users can learn the system with little or no training.

IBM Lotus Workplace Messaging provides a cost-effective way to extend an e-mail and messaging infrastructure to all employees (traditional and nontraditional "deskless") with a standards-based solution that is easy to use, scalable, and rich with security features. Enabled by IBM Workplace Client Technology, Lotus Workplace Messaging provides a range of capabilities.

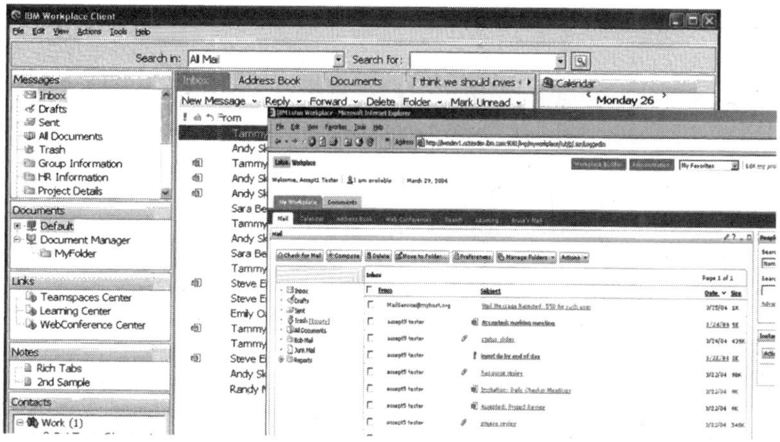

Figure 3.2. Lotus Workplace Messaging.

While Lotus Workplace offers a low cost, standards-based, simple messaging experience for browser users, it now also provides server-managed delivery of a rich client capability for those users who can benefit from an extended set of integrated productivity tools. With the flexibility and capabilities traditionally found in desktop applications, plus the manageability and cost benefits of Web-based applications, the Lotus Workplace Messaging rich client experience provides the best of both worlds.

This provides a simple new alternative for communicating and disseminating information to large numbers of deskless employees (or nontraditional users), and for other employees with more extensive needs, Lotus Workplace Messaging is appropriate. The rich client enables organizations to provide their higher-needs users with productivity-enhancing capabilities, such as disconnected (off-line) use, viewing of attached documents from within applications, drag-and-drop functionality, integrated instant messaging with e-mail, calendaring and scheduling, and much more.

Flexible to support a range of user needs, Lotus Workplace Messaging can help organizations reduce their costs by providing users with simplified access to messaging and application support, along with centralized, no-touch, policy-based provisioning and management of the end-user communities. Supporting the basic principles of the on demand model, Lotus Workplace Messaging is security-rich, scalable, flexible, and adaptable to meet a mix of requirements.

Many employees in industries like manufacturing, retail, distribution, or construction often have limited or no access to their organization's electronic business communications. These employees could include retail clerks, factory floor workers, or construction workers who do not have access to e-mail. This lack of access can make efficiently receiving and responding to critical business information a challenge. For example, delivering by mail the paper printed weekly work schedules, mailing benefits information, or even printing and mailing pay stubs, can be costly, time-consuming, and unproductive. Using the traditional corporate e-mail systems and desktop application environments would be cost prohibitive for many employees that traditionally would not have such systems access. But now, for about the same cost as producing and delivering paper-based payroll stubs, nontraditional users could be provided with access to secure browser-based e-mail systems and a mix of applications that would make them more productive in their roles.

Because not all employees have access to e-mail, many businesses need to provide employees with biweekly pay stubs and often do such by way of printing paper and mailing the pay stub via the postal system. Instead, a company could now provide the Lotus Workplace infrastructure and enable electronic pay stubs for all employees. Businesses can also deliver this function to employees that wouldn't normally have any access to corporate collaborative applications and e-mail, but now can—and all this at an affordable cost.

Organizations need a user-friendly, cost-effective way to communicate with these deskless employees. And IT administrators need a solution that is reliable, security rich, and easy to manage and deploy; a solution that coexists alongside the current messaging infrastructure, allowing them to leverage IT investments. The same organizations may have employees who require extended productivity features for their role. These employees can use Lotus Workplace Messaging rich client capabilities.

Lotus Workplace Messaging can also help lower cost of ownership by integrating with existing directory and messaging infrastructures. Leveraging current IT investment is critical to help reduce costs and simplify deployment. Lotus Workplace Messaging enables you to integrate with any standards-based messaging infrastructure, including IBM Lotus Domino or Microsoft Exchange, by using industry standards like LDAP and SMTP. One can use an existing third-party LDAP directory, such as Domino Directory, Microsoft Exchange, or Microsoft Active Directory, to easily connect Lotus Workplace Messaging to an existing directory infrastructure. This eliminates the need to invest in a separate internal directory with redundant attributes, and lets a business leverage existing LDAP capabilities and knowledge so they do not need to spend more money or time learning new skills. A standard LDAP directory also enables transparent merging of an existing messaging solution, like Lotus Domino or Microsoft Exchange, and the new Lotus Workplace Messaging server so existing and new users can communicate electronically with each other by locating e-mail addresses across multiple LDAP directories.

Enabled by IBM's Workplace Client Technology, Lotus Workplace Messaging delivers on the needs of organizations wanting a rich user experience for increased productivity. The dynamic provisioning and low- or no-touch deployment model makes it easy to deploy and manage. Applications that provide collaboration capabilities can be installed, updated, and uninstalled through policies administered from the server. Dynamic provisioning can be setup so administrators can push down, update, and pull back capabilities, such as instant messaging, as well as specific application rights like editor versus reader rights. Off-line support allows employees to continue working when disconnected from the network.

Integrated instant messaging has the ability to save conversations and is rich with security features so that the information exchanged is protected. The security of instant messaging is essential for the business that wants to keep confidential chat sessions from being made public.

There are several useful mail-related functions, such as the ability to print mail and calendar information, full-text searching, and nested folder management for categorizing and organizing mail.

If you install and license other Lotus Workplace products, there is good integration automatically provided among the various products. For example, the Lotus Workplace Messaging product integrates well with the Lotus Workplace Documents product, enabling a way to archive e-mail, and locate document attachments.

The personal contacts list can utilize the presence and awareness and integrate that with the mail system. This allows for more productive communication options among users. Sometimes a quick instant message chat session is a more productive response to an e-mail than a reply e-mail would be.

Another component of LWP Messaging is called *Activity Explorer*, which combines the ad hoc power of e-mail and chat with the rich collaboration features of shared work environments. This runs in IBM Workplace Client Technology and represents a new form of collaboration. Users can collaborate and share their work using five types of shared objects: Shared Message, Persistent Chat, Shared File, Shared Screen, Shared Folder. These shared conversations, documents, and objects are organized into structured "activity threads" for easy viewing and tracking, which means users no longer need to sift through an e-mail inbox or search for saved instant messages (if they were saved at all) to find information related to a given project or topic. More details of this component are discussed in Chapter 4, "A New Approach to Collaboration."

Lotus Workplace Team Collaboration

When working as a team, it's important to have available the tools that enable the team to work effectively together, whether or not they are in the same location. Every task force that is set up to accomplish a task needs to share information, assign tasks, work as a team, and collaborate. IBM Lotus Workplace Team Collaboration is an integrated environment that provides instant messaging, presence awareness, Web conferencing, and customizable Team Spaces.

Lotus Workplace Team Collaboration (see Figure 3.3) helps individuals, teams, and entire organizations increase business communication efficiency and improve productivity. The cost of this product is affordable to deliver this type of function to all users within a community, not just the high-value users.

This type of environment creates a sense of community and can provide a cost-effective way to communicate, conduct training, and host departmental

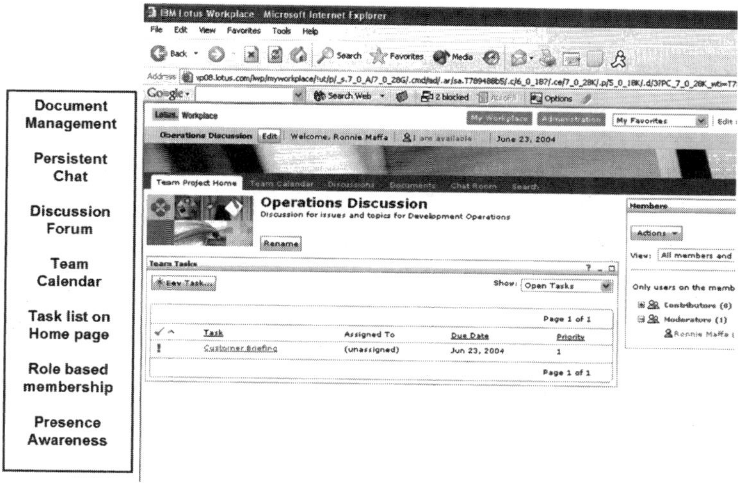

Figure 3.3. Lotus Workplace Team Collaboration.

meetings with users in multiple remote locations participating. Instant, anytime access to people and information minimizes the cycles associated with e-mail and voice mail "tag," and complex searches for timely information.

Lotus Workplace Team Collaboration blends real-time with asynchronous collaboration, enabling users to have access to instant messaging and presence awareness. This lets users know, in advance, whether a person or group of people is available. This includes presence awareness management, contact list management and portlets, multiway text messaging, and statistics management capabilities. Lotus Workplace Team Collaboration is easier and more cost effective to install, use, maintain, and upgrade than using separate products for each function. You can leverage this solution to help reduce the complexity of your IT infrastructure.

Users can participate in Web conferences (see Figure 3.4) via a browser; there is no client download required. Users can schedule, prepare, attend, and search Web conferences. This features a My Meeting summary view and a summary of active meetings. Users can easily control who creates a meeting, lock the meeting, and even eject participants. The Web Conferencing function provides live meeting capabilities. The moderator of a meeting can share presentations and give participants the option to download meeting materials. Although users may be geographically dispersed team members, this can help create a

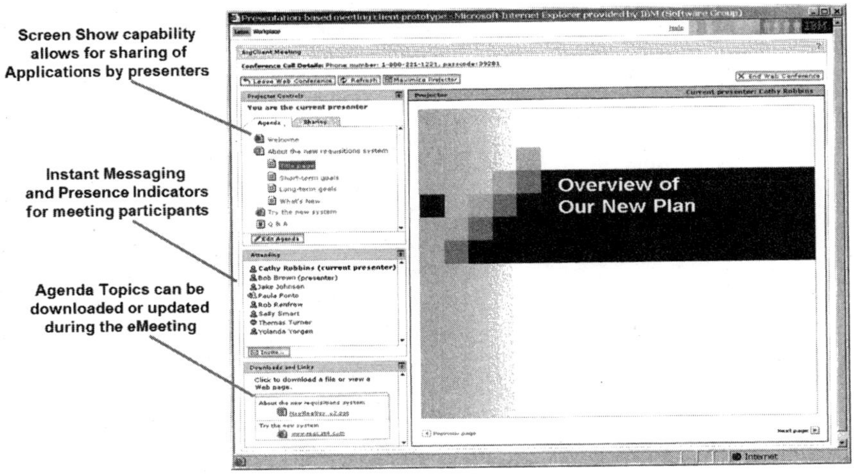

Figure 3.4. Lotus Workplace Web Conferencing.

sense of community. The Web Conferencing provides for user interface customization, multiple moderators, and hand-off controls. There is a conversion of a presentation to a more efficient format for distribution of a chart over the Internet done with high-quality conversion and slide transitions.

Team Spaces provide capabilities that can be customized to suit a team's particular requirements. Team Spaces include self-service management that allows an authorized member to create, customize, and navigate personal Team Spaces and invite team members to collaborate about projects or initiatives. Team Spaces allow users to start and maintain discussion forums and perform document management functions, such as document locking and creating productivity portlets. The self-service management allows users to create, navigate, and search the Team Spaces. The member management and self-service area is designed for gathering people to participate in collaborative activities. Team Space policies allow for the management and monitoring of inactivity and size quotas.

The library functions provide a centralized location for documents, along with built-in methods for tracking changes and comments made by team members. Authorized members have the ability to read, edit, and delete documents, as well as to create and delete folders.

Discussion forums can be used to provide Web-based discussion forums, or a forum within a forum, and allow members to engage in threaded discussions.

The search capability gives authorized users the ability to perform searches within a single Team Space or across Team Spaces. Users also have the ability to search Web conferences of which they are members.

There are many prebuilt templates that can be utilized by users, or they can use the Lotus Workplace Builder to create new ones. For example, Team Discussion, Document Library, Project, Persistent Chat Rooms, and Team calendar with Web Conferencing are already provided in formats predesigned by Lotus. This is good because it provides a fast way to get started using the Lotus Workplace products in a user community. Over time, as an organization becomes more familiar with the environment and tools, they'll want to enable administrators to build new templates and take advantage of the component-based approach of building collaborative applications.

Lotus Workplace Builder helps you easily customize Team Spaces to meet industry-specific or business process-specific requirements. It doesn't require the users to have programming skills. With the Builder, users can create, edit templates, and change template details and properties. There is the ability to create, reorder, and delete pages; choose page content; page layout; and permissions. Users can define and control membership. There is forms management and an ability to manage the configuration of each application component.

When a new Team Space, Web conference, or document library is created, many steps are automatically processed for the end user. Let's consider the steps required for the creating of a Team Space using the default template. When a user creates a default Team Space, only two questions are asked, the name of the Team Space and description (and the latter is optional!). After submitting this, Lotus Workplace Team Collaboration must create the appropriate portal pages dynamically, place the portlets on the page as defined in the template, create the document repositories for the Team Space content and for the documents that will be stored there, create the search index for the Team Space, create a default membership list, and propagate the appropriate portal access control to all of these objects. This only takes a few seconds. Imagine having to do this manually! Not only would it take longer, but it also introduces the possibility of error.

A key imperative for becoming an on demand business is improving employee productivity. Team collaboration is essential to improving employee productivity in terms of communication, responsiveness, and sharing information. For both large and small organizations, these types of collaboration can take time for users to become comfortable and productive with, so it's important to start as soon as possible to help achieve a faster adoption and breakthrough in productivity.

For organizations that have already implemented such types of capabilities for the traditional high-value users, the Lotus Workplace family now provides a way to enable all users within an organization to participate. These advanced services complement the robust capabilities of other IBM technologies, such as IBM Lotus Notes, IBM Lotus Domino, IBM Lotus Instant Messaging and Web Conferencing (IBM Lotus Sametime), and IBM Lotus Team Workplace (IBM Lotus QuickPlace) software.

As with all Lotus Workplace products, Lotus Workplace Team Collaboration offers a standards-based team collaboration solution that can leverage existing IT skills and technologies. This integrates with existing supported infrastructures like IBM Lotus Domino using open standards including J2EE, LDAP, and HTML. Lotus Workplace Team Collaboration embraces standards-based security features for authentication of users, confidentiality of content, and integrity of the information data.

Lotus Workplace Documents

In most businesses today, e-mail systems have become an essential element of their critical business processes. In other words, if they shut off their e-mail systems, they would be shutting down their business. A common problem that businesses face is the fact that in some situations people often use their e-mail system as a place to store documents, as if it were a repository. The storage capacity requirements for such situations becomes enormous and often it is also a major burden on the network traffic.

IBM Lotus Workplace Documents (see Figure 3.5) helps organizations by providing intuitive document organizing, sharing, handling, and editing capabilities. This provides library services for check-in and check-out, versioning, and document locking. The enterprise-level document management capabilities facilitate document lifecycle management. This helps organizations to protect their information assets while simplifying their ability to organize and share important documents in a secure environment across the organization.

Accessible via a Web browser or via the rich client, Lotus Workplace Documents provides capabilities to help users complete their daily tasks as related to documents more efficiently. Lotus Workplace Documents also facilitates the process of document lifecycle management, from collaborative authoring to archival, while simplifying the ability to find, store, and manage important documents, including spreadsheets, presentations, drawings, e-mails, and others.

By integrating well with other Lotus Workplace products, the Lotus Workplace Documents product provides organizations collaboration by way of instant messaging and awareness, e-mail archiving from Lotus Workplace

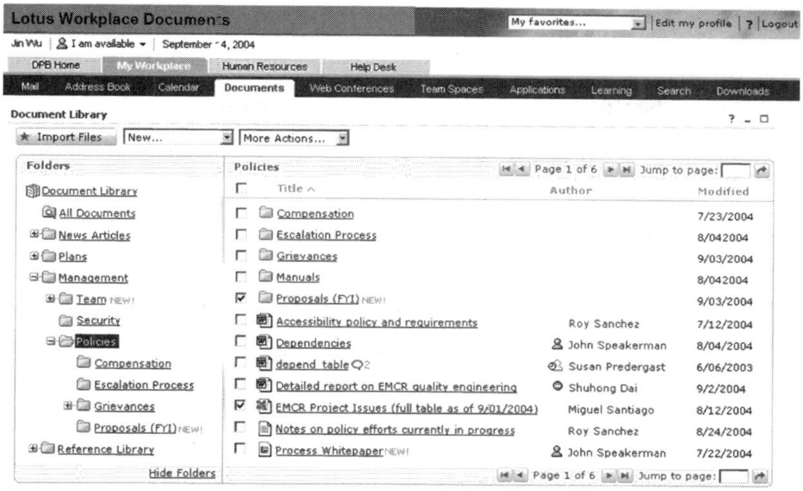

Figure 3.5. Lotus Workplace Documents.

Messaging, and access to portal document libraries. There is also optional integration with DB2 Content Manager as a repository.

Lotus Workplace Builder provides the ability for administrators to easily customize document library portlets to meet industry or business process-specific requirements.

The rich client environment for Lotus Workplace Documents also includes rich document editors for word processing, spreadsheets, and presentations. The dynamic client provisioning enables disconnected (off-line) support, secure encrypted local document store, and server/client synchronization.

Organizational effectiveness can be improved by providing centralized, consistent management of documents and information. Lotus Workplace Documents promotes collaboration via support of awareness and chat among document authors, editors, and owners. It speeds decisions because you can reuse information that is stored in shared documents. It eliminates wasteful recreation of documentation or work based on incorrect or outdated documentation. And it provides a secure environment and synchronous experience for end users to create, import, edit, and save documents, presentations, and spreadsheets within an integrated rich client experience.

This rich client environment can also help improve the productivity of employees with infrequent access to your company's network by way of the ability to work off-line (disconnected) using a secure local store. It can help lower the total cost of ownership through infrastructure simplification, using a common administration model, a common place to deploy collaborative document management capabilities to end users, with low- to no-touch deployment model coupled with central policy-based management of the end user's desktop environment.

Existing investments in Lotus software are planned to be carried forward to comparable components and capabilities within the Lotus Workplace family of integrated collaborative applications. Organizations with WebSphere Portal already implemented can continue with WebSphere Portal and access Lotus Domino data via portlets. They can then implement Lotus Workplace collaboration products to extend the business integration of WebSphere Portal by introducing rich collaborative capabilities and functionality. If starting a fresh and new environment, an organization can use Lotus Workplace products as the foundation for a collaborative infrastructure.

IBM Workplace Project Scheduler

IBM Workplace project planner (see Figure 3.6) is a component of Lotus Workplace Documents that enables the tracking and reporting of project data with

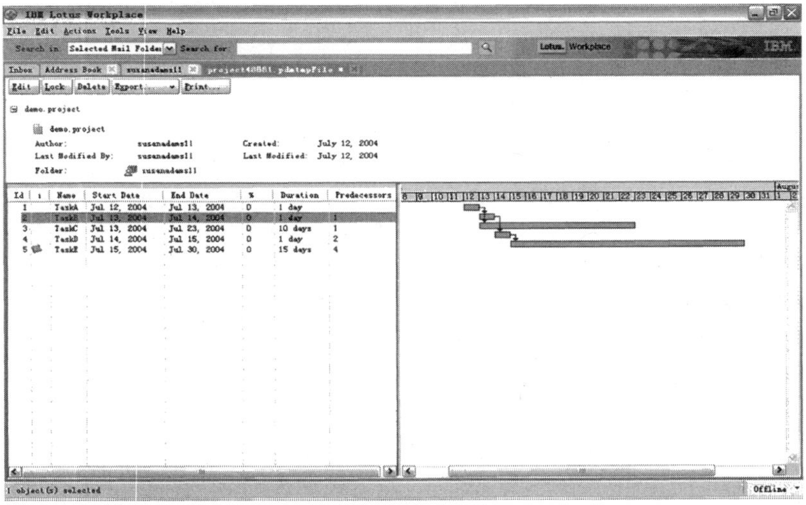

Figure 3.6. Lotus Workplace Documents (Project Scheduler).

a Gantt chart view. It is delivered as a rich client component and packaged with LWP Documents. Project managers can add project tasks and resources, assign tasks to resources, create sub and summary tasks, and link dependent tasks. There is the ability to import and export data from Microsoft Project XML files.

IBM Workplace Data Access

IBM Workplace Data Access (see Figure 3.7) is another component of LWP Documents that allows users to set up simple queries based on certain criteria and parameters. This enables users to work with the data more easily, and create WYSIWYG reports. IBM Workplace Data Access leverages IBM Workplace Client Technology for server-managed client, dynamic provisioning to users, off-line and synchronization. This utilizes the secure, encrypted local data store of the IBM Workplace Client.

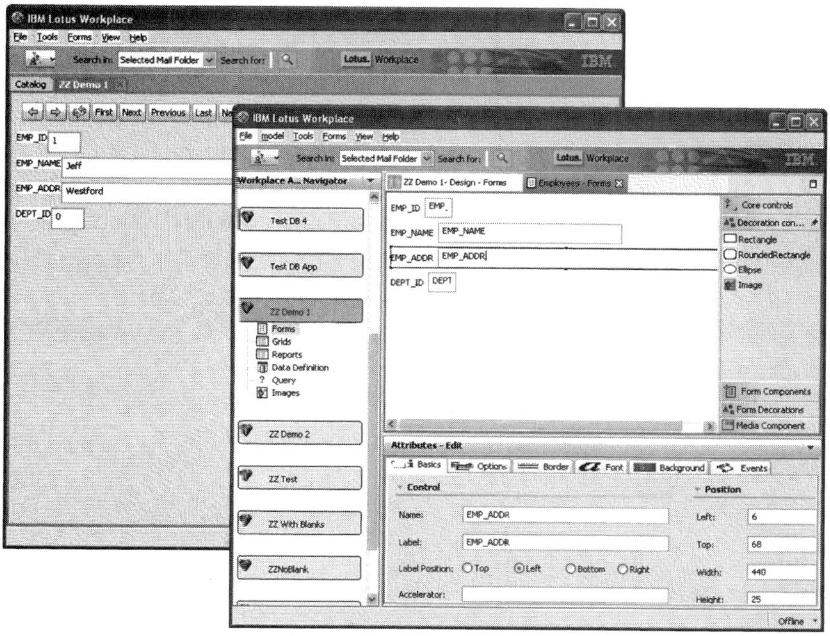

Figure 3.7. Lotus Workplace Documents (Data Access).

Lotus Workplace Collaborative Learning

Skill development is essential to success within any organization. Providing online education and managing a role-based education implementation can help achieve greater results in terms of productivity and career development targets. Both traditional computer users within an organization and nontraditional users have need for skill development. Flight attendants may need to be recertified on certain procedures or update their skills about a particular jet before being able to fly it. Manufacturing plant workers may need to register for and take a series of training courses as new designs of products are being implemented. Cashiers at a retail department store may need to learn the latest information on how to detect counterfeit currency on newly issued bills. Bus drivers may need to annually refresh their skills in emergency procedures.

Many nontraditional users can now be given access to learning systems and have such integrated with other collaborative services. For example, when an employee is given a promotion, they may be sent an e-mail indicating such, provisioned and given access to specific applications related to that promotion. The system could be setup so that before the employee is able to access that application for the first time, they are registered in an online training class. Once the training is completed successfully, the access to the application is granted.

Lotus Workplace Collaborative Learning (see Figure 3.8) is the next release in the Lotus Learning Management System, which helps users manage educational programs, activities, and resources more efficiently. This learning solution helps organizations by keeping track of who has taken required training. It also helps educate and train employees cost-effectively, and enables the delivery of role-based, self-service online learning to every desktop or mobile user in an organization. Students can find the learning resources they need, work toward professional certification, and take courses in their own office and at their own pace.

With Lotus Workplace Collaborative Learning, in-house experts can quickly create repeatable, consistent courses that employees can use to train themselves on such crucial topics as company best practices, business processes, and policies. It is useful for industry and government organizations to communicate and inform about regulations and requirements, and market or industry changes, trends, and issues.

Lotus Workplace Collaborative Learning delivers learning resources in a portal-style user interface that's personalized for each user, based on his or her role in the enterprise; the user can access the portal from wherever he or she happens to be.

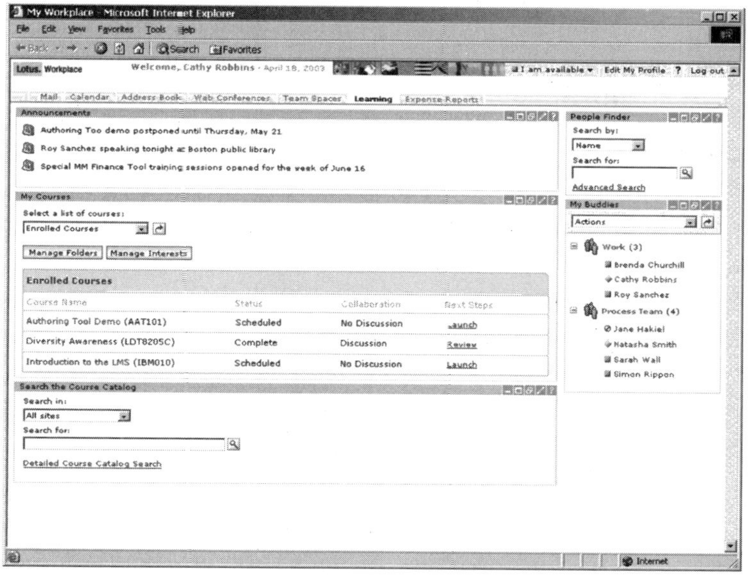

Figure 3.8. Lotus Workplace Collaborative Learning.

When integrated into the Lotus Notes client, IBM WebSphere Portal, Lotus Virtual Classroom, or the Lotus Workplace environment, Lotus Workplace Collaborative Learning lets users seamlessly combine just-in-time learning with collaborative applications such as awareness, instant messaging, calendaring and scheduling, and workflows. All this enables faster response to unexpected opportunities, customer demands, and external threats.

IBM Lotus Workplace Collaborative Learning provides a modular, standards-based, extensible learning-management system. It is designed to streamline organizational learning activities and integrate online, personalized learning resources on the user's desktop. Its support for industry standards, availability in multiple languages, and disconnected use allows mobile and remote workers to access courseware libraries wherever they are located, whenever it is convenient for them.

Lotus Workplace Collaborative Learning includes all the functions of the Lotus Learning Management System, enhanced with a portlet-based student user interface and integration with the Lotus Workplace environment. It manages and schedules both classroom-based and electronic learning activities, resources, and courseware across an enterprise and provides powerful administrative tools for managing student enrollments. Lotus Workplace Collaborative Learning helps organizations tailor their training programs to be more cost effective and responsive to an organization's needs.

Lotus Workplace Collaborative Learning has a portlet-based student user interface (UI) and searchable catalog that deliver online learning resources to a user's desktop. The student UI is a powerful productivity tool that enables employees to self-manage their learning activities, enroll in desired classes, and quickly access the information they need. The portlets' content can be customized to suit a user's job role, industry, and profile, delivering an appropriate learning environment to each user.

By delivering context-driven learning resources that are personalized, relevant, and pervasive (available any time, anywhere), Lotus Workplace Collaborative Learning integrates learning into workers' day-to-day activities, enabling them to improve their skills and response to job requirements.

Lotus Workplace Collaborative Learning integrates with other Lotus Workplace products. Integrating Lotus Workplace Collaborative Learning and Lotus Workplace Messaging provides calendar integration and the ability to send notifications to a user's inbox. Integration with Lotus Workplace Team Collaboration enables students to use instant messaging during online courses and create more sophisticated collaboration features (tasks, Web conferences) within the learning environment.

Lotus Workplace Collaborative Learning is also a full-featured, end-to-end, standards-compliant learning management system with an easy-to-use courseware development and management authoring tool, customizable reporting, and powerful administration functions. The product's customizable reporting on training activities is often an important component of structuring certification programs and for complying with new industry and government regulations.

The authoring tool enables you to create and deliver your own customized courseware for projects such as new product introductions, customer training, or teaching "best practices" to workers. Because of its open architecture and support for industry standards, Lotus Workplace Collaborative Learning integrates well with your third-party back-office systems, such as SAP and PeopleSoft. In addition, it supports industry standards such as Shareable Content Object Reference Model (SCORM) and Aviation Industry CBT Committee (AICC), which provides compatibility with existing courseware libraries. Organizations can use third-party developed courseware from IBM Business Partners.

IBM Lotus Workplace Collaborative Learning can help deliver up-to-date learning resources to dispersed audiences, efficiently meet ongoing training requirements, and measure the results and effectiveness of training deliverables.

Organizations can address regulatory compliance challenges by tracking and reporting worker training activities.

Workplace Builder (Templates)

In any organization, there are various levels of skills among users, administrators, and developers. Building new applications and creating templates of applications for others to use is essentially how the business transformations and business process ideas are put into practice. Having tools that make this task easy while also providing a reliable, functional, and rapid deployment is key to the effectiveness of an environment and its overall success.

Workplace Builder (see Figure 3.9) provides the ability for users and administrators to create templates and applications that work within the Lotus Workplace environment. Creating a workplace based on templates, using the template editor, makes the development and reliable deployment of application function relatively easy for any size organization.

Lotus provides many templates to begin with, and, if you don't like the templates Lotus provides, you can create your own.

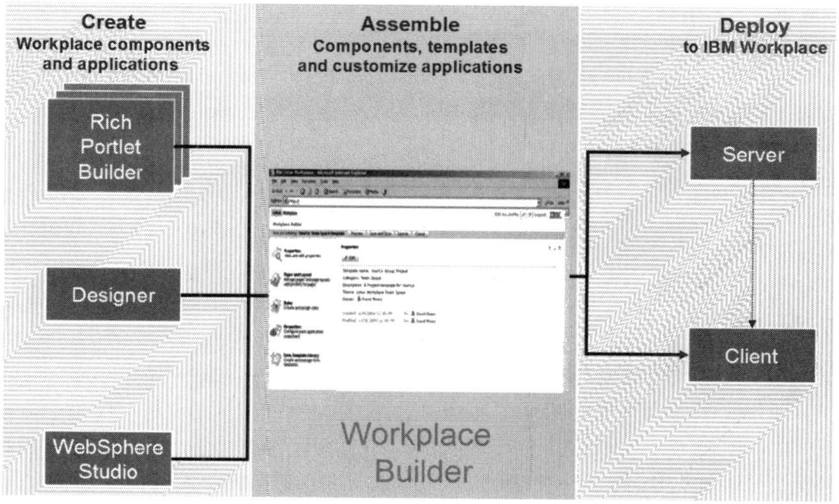

Figure 3.9. Workplace Builder.

Remember that the strategy and model of the IBM Workplace and Lotus Workplace products fully embrace the IBM software strategy of componentization. It's essentially the idea of building components and enabling an environment in which the components can be shared, reused, and applied in a mix of ways that best address a business need and application design.

Workplace Builder (see Figure 3.10) is a method for assembling components. It provides the ability to assemble existing portlets into an application. Programming by assembly without coding means that the end-user population can put together applications relatively easily and this makes for a more rapid deployment. Users can customize running Workplace applications using a browser. This self-service nature of the application-building process means that it removes burden from IT staff to make simple modifications.

Users can create application templates that are immediately deployed on the server and are controlled by policy and access permissions. This means that no deployment step is necessary. The self-service aspect lowers the costs of creating and deploying new applications. Templates can be imported and exported from the server repository. This enables users to move the template from one system to another. Template permissions are determined by the template owner. They can limit who can use a template and who can edit the template, and this provides control over deployment to the end-user population.

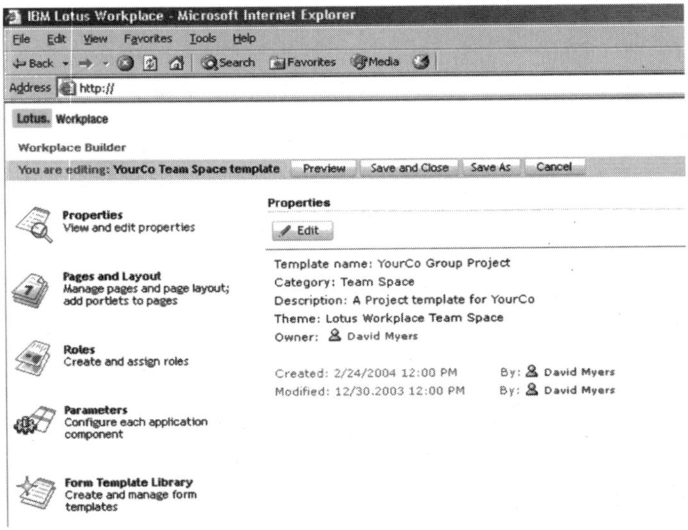

Figure 3.10. Workplace Builder.

People can create new templates from an existing application. For example, as team members develop best practices and customize an application, they would want to save the customized application as a reusable asset. This makes it possible for users to save and share successful work practices for others in the organization.

Community roles are used to aggregate component access roles into one application-specific role name. Use the membership portlet to assign people to roles in the running application. For example, a project manager role can be defined with certain access rights to various components, or the home page has reader access, the document library has author access, the membership administration has owner access. Application designers can create user-friendly names for roles specific to a business domain. For example, "sales manager," "teacher," "executive," etc.

Workplace portlets can expose their parameters to the tool, which can then present them in a single, unified user interface. Template editors control parameter default values and whether they can be modified at run time by end users. This improves productivity by simplifying the user experience for customizing both templates and applications. It provides IT control when desired because template editors can lock down parameter values, ensuring that the application runs as intended.

The form builder lets end users create simple forms for their applications through a wizard-like interface. The form template library is accessed via the Workplace Builder link in the masthead, which is controlled by policy. Simple tasks like creating basic forms can be performed by end users, without involving IT resources, thus lowering the cost and time to a solution.

Administration for Lotus Workplace

Lotus Workplace is administered through a Web-based, policy management system that enables a policy framework (see Figure 3.11). This is where IBM has significantly simplified the administration of a portal-based solution. Instead of having to create access control for objects on the system, for each user or group, the policy management system allows for the simple selection of the features required. The policy management system then communicates with the portal to propagate any changes required.

First, the licensing of the Lotus Workplace products is controlled by the policy system (see Figure 3.12). When installing any Lotus Workplace product, the complete infrastructure is installed. In fact, currently, even though you can purchase any of the Lotus Workplace products individually, they are really all

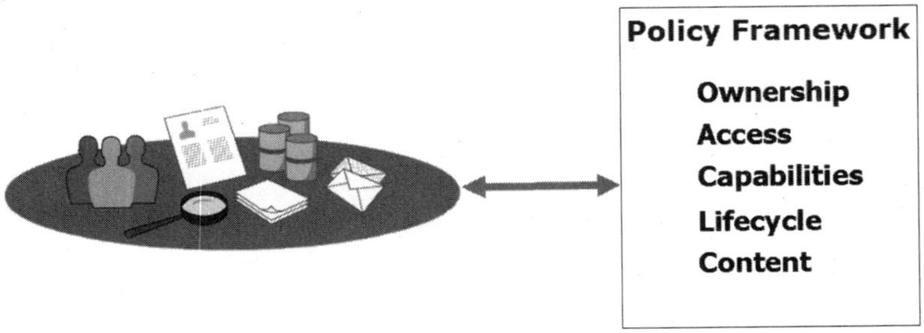

Figure 3.11. Managing Workplaces.

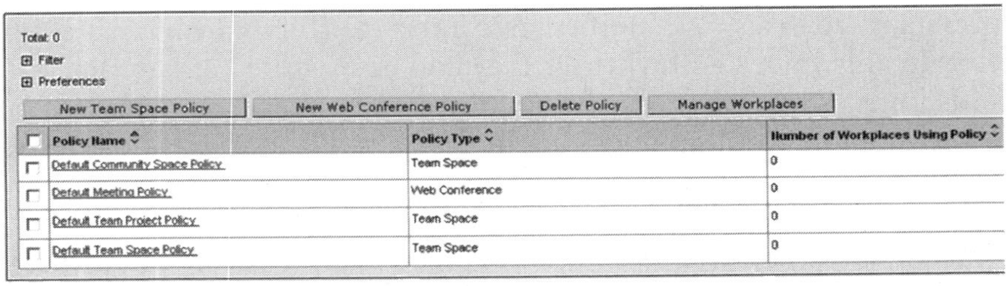

Figure 3.12. Policy-based administration.

the same code. The appropriate application is simply provisioned by modifying the license policy. Today, this is done on an honor system, but in the future this capability could be managed by a call center application.

Individual user policies are then created to control what features of the products that you want to provision to users or groups. For example, one group of users can be enabled for messaging, calendar and instant messaging only, whereas others may have access only to Team Spaces. The Web-based interface makes it simple and easy to create these policies. This allows for a mix-and-match scenario. You can purchase the individual Lotus Workplace products by the number of users required for each. Then the policies can be created to control the number of users that have access to each function.

Policies can also be created to control specific Workplace components, such as Team Spaces, Web conferences, and document libraries. Attributes such as size limits, inactivity rules, and the like can be applied to specific groups to control how Lotus Workplace applications are created. For example, a document library created by the "executive" group may have different capabilities than one created by the "staff" group. This allows the IT organization the freedom to delegate the capability to created Workplace applications while still placing certain controls on them as well.

IBM Workplace Web Content Management

An organization's Web site is a presentation of the corporate image. Often the image of an organization can be damaged because of a lack of Web site controls. Many organizations experience problems with their Web site content being posted without proper authorization or over time the content becoming outdated. Often the people who have responsibilities for managing information and content that could be useful to post on a company Web site don't necessarily have the technical skills to do so.

IBM Workplace Web Content Management (IWWCM) is illustrated in Figure 3.13; this product provides workflow process control and approval. Web Content Management helps solve IT and webmaster bottlenecks by placing content creation and management in the hands of content experts, who can author once and publish everywhere the same content on the Web site. It helps improve the Web content management process by providing a rapid content deployment capability with a point-and-click interface.

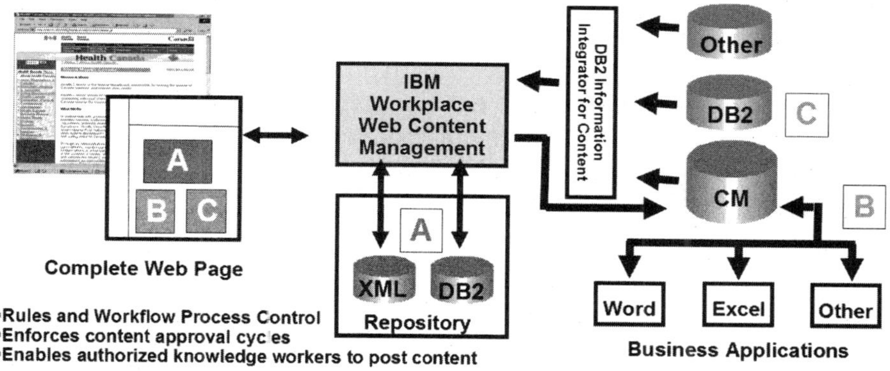

Figure 3.13. IBM Workplace Web Content Management.

With IWWCM you can keep your site up to date, locate who owns content and whom to contact for updates, and meet the content needs of a wide variety of site audiences. Web Content Management enables the reuse of content stored in other systems and the ability to publish it on multiple sites. This will help reduce the cost of content development and management by streamlining the content-management process with built-in lifecycle workflows.

IBM Workplace Web Content Management can be a central process workflow collaboration hub and pull information and content from a variety of sources. It has good integration with the WebSphere Portal and content repositories, such as DB2 Content Manager. Support for XML and integration with database environments enable a variety of ways for content to be stored and retrieved so that it can be available for knowledge workers to access and process. Building templates for how content should look enables corporate standards to be adhered to easily.

In addition, businesses often need to meet regulations of the marketplace and governmental requirements. The integrity of the process demands strict and auditable content management, which IWWCM provides.

With an increase in the use of portal-based applications also comes a time-consuming, manual process of content creation. Web content management typically requires specific programming skills. Publishing Web content across your Internet, intranet, and extranet assets often becomes the job of the webmaster and IT employees. Any delay in keeping up with the demand of content deployment to customers, partners, and users can block access to critical business information.

IBM Workplace Web Content Management can deploy across existing infrastructures to leverage current IT investments. It helps lower administration and development costs with a standards-based, scalable, security-rich environment.

As illustrated in Figure 3.14, IWWCM is a flexible, scalable, and configurable Web content management system with a portlet-style front end that seamlessly integrates into the Workplace environment. It is an open standards-compliant product that gives workers an instant way to find and personalize essential information to be posted to Web sites.

Instead of waiting indefinitely for it to be extracted from a multitude of repositories, systems, and obscure applications by overworked developers, knowledge workers can extract information easily from such repositories and create their own content portlets fast. The collaborative environment makes it easy for users of all levels to work together and complete review and approval workflow processes.

Content personalization support dynamically delivers content that is relevant to the users and their roles. With rapid portal development, portlets are

Figure 3.14. IBM Workplace Web Content Management.

created using a simple point-and-click interface within WebSphere Portal Server, removing the need for Java development skills. Users create, manage, and publish information straight into the portal.

IBM Workplace for Business Controls and Reporting

Businesses and organizations across all industries and throughout the world are facing intensifying scrutiny by governments for possible fraud and abuse violations. Regulatory and accreditation bodies have also tightened operational requirements. An integrated, comprehensive compliance program is a necessity.

IBM Workplace for Business Controls and Reporting provides the knowledge and information management, and portal and collaboration infrastructures to help address internal business control and reporting requirements. This can provide top management with visibility into the effectiveness of a company's internal business controls. Document processes support the identification of risks and controls and facilitate the evaluation of the effectiveness of the controls. Top executives can receive summaries and a compliance overview for their organization.

There are two phases to the development and implementation of a compliance program: first, developing the overall program structure and second, operationalizing the program. An organization will only be able to demonstrate its compliance program is effective when the program has been integrated into the day-to-day operations of every department. An effective program creates an environment that reinforces the commitment to compliance while providing a framework to identify and correct potential issues of noncompliance. The compliance program should not impede or replace the organizational processes currently in place, but rather should compliment and enhance them in order to create a more effective and efficient operation.

Within the United States, the Sarbanes-Oxley Act of 2002 ("SOX-404," Management Assessment of Internal Controls) was signed into law by President Bush on July 30, 2002, with a goal to place more accountability on those who make decisions within public companies by increasing emphasis on controls. The government has mandated that all publicly traded companies comply with the mandate by 2004.

Business content is all interrelated and has a lifecycle. A key step in your efforts to comply with requirements regarding management assessment of internal controls is tying multiple repositories together, even if they are from different vendors. The fundamental issue is the need to have control over content, to know where it is, and to manage it effectively.

This solution helps provide a platform for an organization's business reporting process and an organized approach to gathering information about business controls, including controls over financial reporting.

As illustrated in Figure 3.15, the view of the end user can be customized to the role of the user. It provides an automated work flow to help document and evaluate internal business controls. Executive dashboards can allow management the ability to actively monitor the internal controls environment on a continuous real-time basis, helping management to assess the effectiveness of a company's internal business controls.

Document management, collaboration, training, and records management functions are all integrated with a single repository. The content repository forms the foundation for organizing control activities, disseminating information, gathering the information required to help evaluate risk, and monitor the internal control system. The knowledge-gathering and notification capabilities can help you to discover internal and external risks quickly to help you make timely and well-informed decisions.

This solution also reaches across geographic and organizational boundaries for consistent reporting. It incorporates KPMG expertise, which helps leverage KPMG's industry insights and knowledge of internal control processes and prac-

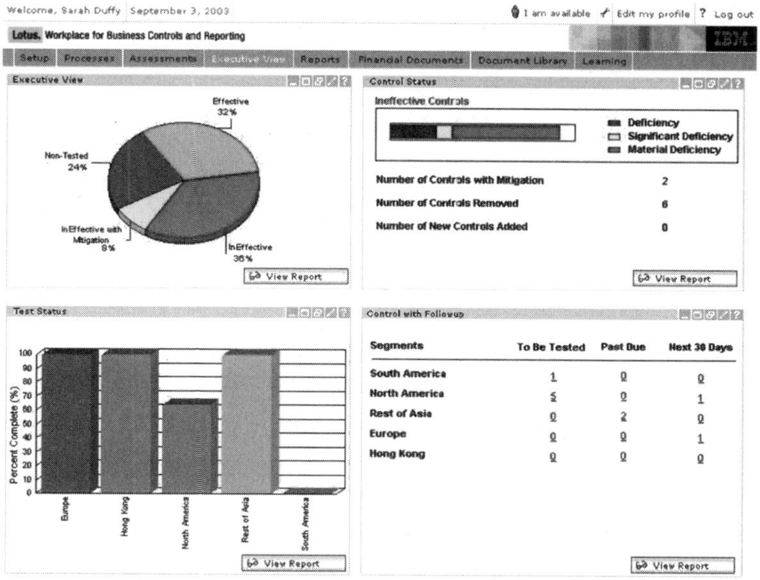

Figure 3.15. IBM Workplace for Business Controls and Reporting.

tices. This is done using the KPMG Control Catalogs, available directly from KPMG at a separate charge.

The IBM Workplace for Business Controls and Reporting provides a foundation that will assist in an organization's efforts to assess its financial reporting in response to Section 404 of the Sarbanes-Oxley Act. This offering can help companies gather and monitor information about controls in a more consistent and organized manner. This Web-based, end-to-end solution can help provide users with greater visibility into a company's financial processes across the enterprise.

IBM's software experience and KPMG's advice and knowledge of internal control creates a comprehensive offering. This is a role-based solution that provides a platform and a consistent, organized approach helping to gain visibility into internal controls to quickly identify issues and help mitigate risks. It can help make it easier for people to communicate and collaborate with presence awareness and instant messaging. This user-friendly navigation support allows users to quickly complete control tasks for greater focus on core business. It provides audit trails and archiving to help ensure process and document integrity.

Embedded workflow helps reduce the risk of accidental errors by streamlining user reviews and approvals. This solution is built on proven technology and is based on open standards. Built on open Java 2 Platform, Enterprise Edition (J2EE) standards, IBM Workplace for Business Controls and Reporting enables you to implement a modular component-based solution. Businesses can tailor their own company's control assessment process to match their specific needs, and then to disperse requests to report on these points of control to the operational units.

IBM Workplace Services Express

IBM Workplace Services Express (WSE) provides a portal framework that is affordable for small and mid-sized organizations to implement. As illustrated in Figure 3.16, WSE is easy to install. It works on both Microsoft Windows and Linux operating systems. It comes with prebuilt portlets and integrated document management capabilities. Users can view, edit, search, categorize, approve, and subscribe to documents.

IBM Workplace Services Express also includes productivity components to provide document editing and viewing capabilities. These components enable portal users to view and edit simple documents, spreadsheets, and presentations stored in an integrated document manager—without the need to install client-side software or browser plug-ins.

Just like large businesses, small and mid-sized businesses also have the need to provide a community environment for their employees, partners, and customers to communicate and connect with. Smaller organizations need quick and easy-to-deploy environments at a cost that is affordable and within their budgets. IBM Workplace Services Express makes sophisticated portals afford-

Figure 3.16. IBM Workplace Services Express can be up and running in under an hour.

able and provides simplified installation and convenient licensing options. It is available at a per-user or per-processor price, whether for employees or others.

IBM Workplace Services Express enables small and mid-sized businesses, as well as departments within larger companies, to more rapidly deploy business-to-business (B2B), business-to-consumer (B2C) and business-to-employee (B2E) portals on Microsoft Windows and Linux systems.

IBM Workplace Services Express is based on the same portal framework as the rest of the IBM WebSphere Portal family, and includes IBM WebSphere Application Server Technology and a wide selection of portlets (integration code that connects applications and data to the portal). The integrated document-management capabilities can help employees share information in order to work faster.

This solution will help improve contact with and among users through a single point of access. The IBM Workplace Services Express framework facilitates the integration of portals with applications and data sources. It streamlines management of administration tasks like portal user membership. You can build highly functional portals that provide a convenient, single point of access to applications, rich content, and people. This will help improve employee productivity with efficient access to business processes, such as enterprise resource planning, supply chain management, and customer relationship management systems.

The installation is greatly simplified. Only a few questions need to be answered and in less than an hour the complete infrastructure is installed. The preconfigured installer gets the basic departmental collaborative environment up and running quickly. The system can easily be configured to utilize the LDAP directory within your organization or use the built-in directory if required.

IBM Workplace Services Express offers an option to include integrated user collaboration functions, such as instant messaging, awareness, team rooms, group calendaring, task and milestone tracking, and discussion areas. These technologies enable the creation and customization of individual and shared team work spaces in a central, safe location on the Web. Administrators or end users can manage portal memberships and projects. Portal users can consolidate, organize, and share ideas, content, and tasks. They can develop discussion areas and store project-related documents in convenient, shared libraries to support team access, or assign tasks and track progress.

The Team Space (see Figure 3.17) application allows for various simple portal applications to be assembled for a team's use, such as "Tasks" or a "Team Calendar" into Team Spaces such as "Team Project," "Meeting Space," and "Company Home." Instant messaging and awareness is enabled to allow synchronous communications with other team members.

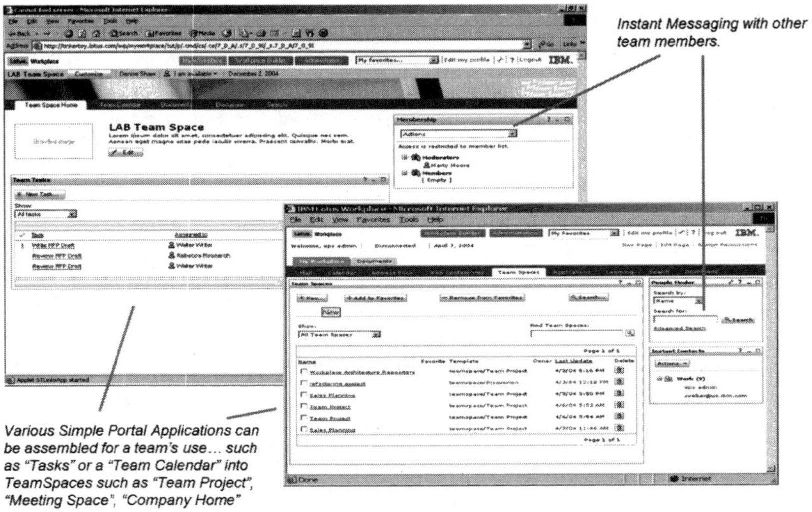

Figure 3.17. IBM Workplace Services Express Team Space application.

The Template Builder (see Figure 3.18) allows the user to create or customize the built-in applications to meet the needs of the organization. Roles, content, and layout can be modified to suit the needs of users, and simple forms can be created to add to the layout.

As well, there is a set of prebuilt "list" type portlets (see Figure 3.19) that maintain lists of interesting things, such as announcements, tasks, events, and contacts, that can be added to any application. Other built-in portlets and portlet-development tools enable the creation of new portals and simplify the addition of new applications to a portal after it has been deployed.

The integrated document management facility allows teams of people to share documents through the portal. This is built with productivity components that provide document editing (see Figures 3.20 and 3.21) and viewing capabilities. These components enable portal users to view and edit simple documents, spreadsheets, and presentations stored in an integrated document manager and without the need to install client-side software or browser plug-ins. A Microsoft Windows extension allows the user to work with portal-managed documents as if they were local files. The files actually reside on the server.

Microsoft Office integration (see Figure 3.22) is enabled through the addition of menus and toolbars within Microsoft Word, Excel, and PowerPoint to

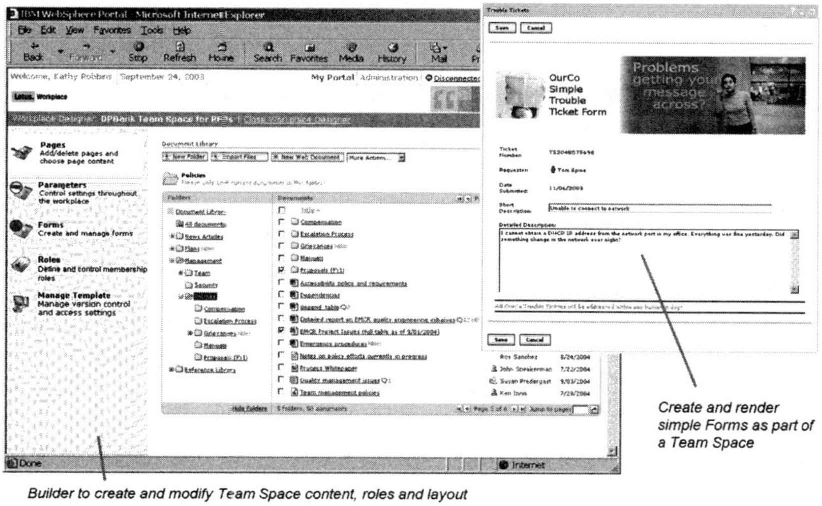

Figure 3.18. IBM Workplace Services Express Template Builder.

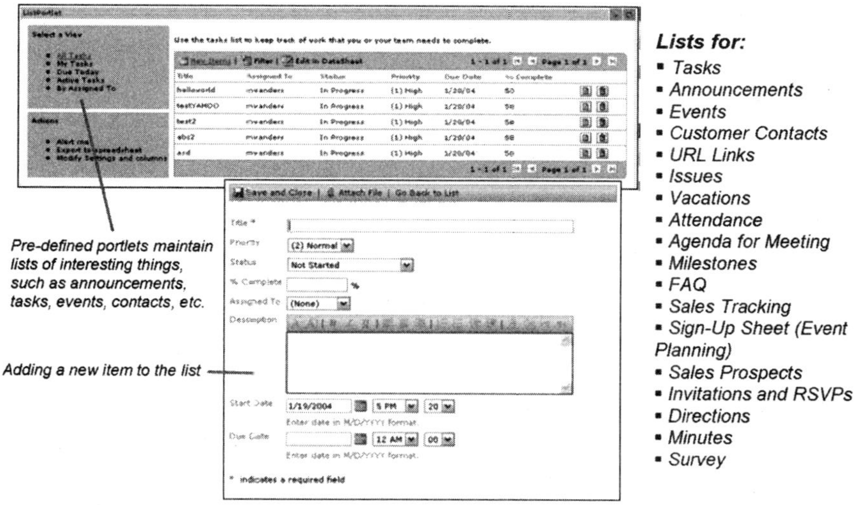

Figure 3.19. IBM Workplace Services Express and the power of simple lists.

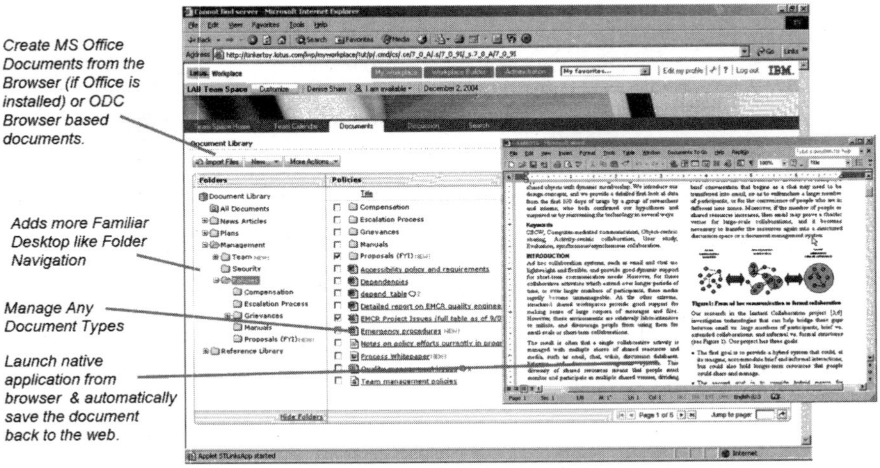

Figure 3.20. IBM Workplace Services Express document management from a browser.

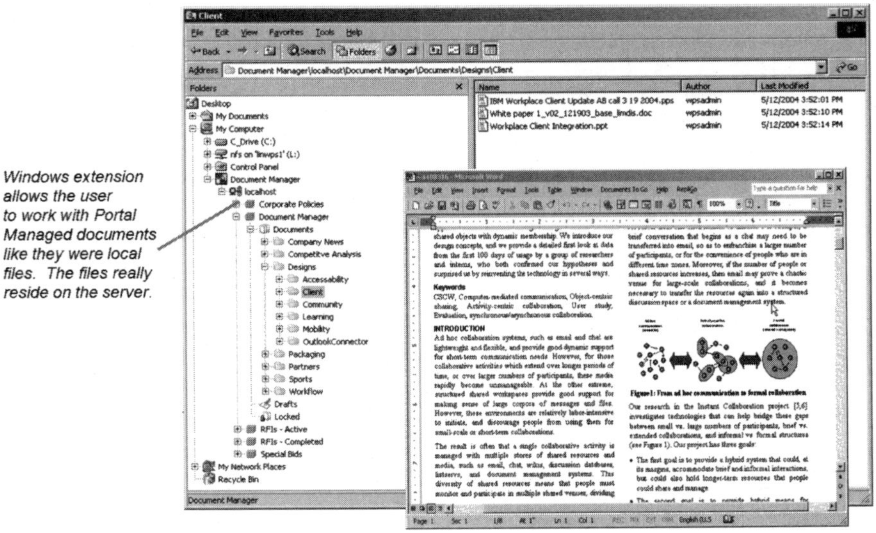

Figure 3.21. IBM Workplace Services Express document management from a desktop.

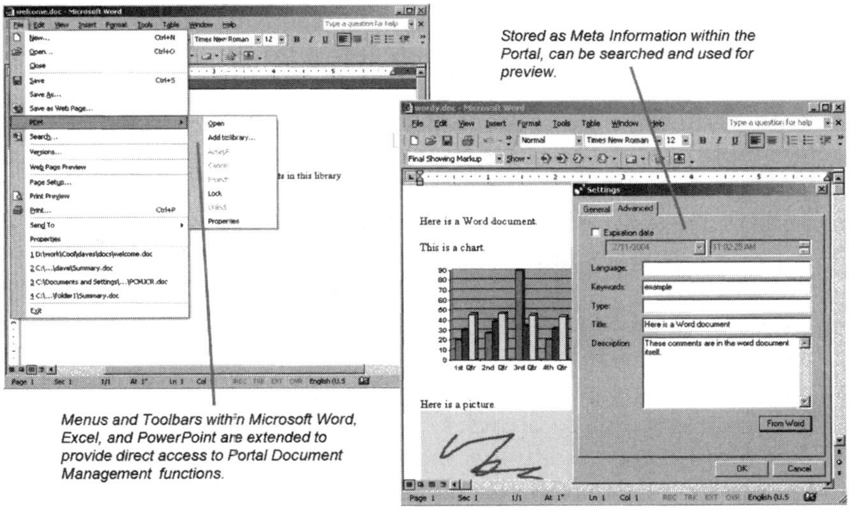

Figure 3.22. IBM Workplace Services Express integration into Microsoft Office.

provide direct access to portal Document Management functions, such as locking, versioning, and so on. The stored meta information within the portal can be searched and used for preview.

IBM Workplace Services Express includes portlets that provide access to frequently used applications, such as e-mail, calendar, and collaboration tools. It also supports single sign-on capabilities so users don't have to sign on separately to every application they use.

IBM Workplace Services Express allows portal users to customize the organization of content within their portal pages to match their needs through a simple drag-and-drop metaphor.

Office Without Office

Many people are impressed when we do demonstrations of editing Microsoft Excel spreadsheets or Microsoft Word documents without having to have Microsoft Office installed on our computer. It is pretty cool, especially when one considers the cost of a typical Lotus Workplace implementation is relatively inexpensive compared with the cost of buying Microsoft Office for everyone in an organization. But, it's important to know how it all works and what can and cannot be done.

One of the features of the IBM Lotus Workplace Documents product is the ability to create and edit standard office documents, such as those used in word processing, spreadsheets, and presentations. It must be noted, however, that the browser support for editing documents is done using the function provided by WebSphere Portal document manager. Although it can import MS Office documents (MS Office Excel, MS Office Word, and MS Office PowerPoint), it can only save them as a PDM (Portal Document Manager) format and only on the server within the document repository. This means a one-way-only import for the browser editing support. But this is still great for many nontraditional users' requirements where browser support is adequate.

For more complete editing support, the LWP Documents rich client function provides the capability of editing such documents. Essentially, this means you have the ability to edit and create Microsoft Office Word documents, Excel spreadsheets, and PowerPoint presentations without actually having Microsoft Office installed on your computer if you use the Lotus Workplace Rich Client and Lotus Workplace Documents. If you use the browser-based editors, it's a one-way import from Microsoft Office to edit such, which is still very useful.

4

A New Approach to Collaboration

Over fifteen years ago, when Lotus introduced Notes/Domino, the "killer app" at the time was Lotus 123 (a spreadsheet application). Interestingly, at that time Lotus didn't know what the next killer app was going to be for team productivity and the collaboration world. In fact, e-mail was just a sample application that came with Notes/Domino. Fifteen years later, we now know e-mail was and still is the killer app in collaboration. E-mail is an essential part of a business. When we look forward and talk about Lotus Workplace and the move toward organizational productivity, we are in the same position of not knowing what exactly the killer app will be for organizational productivity. But we do know that enabling people with a flexible modular environment of services that they can build on will open the door to innovation.

The architecture and technology of Lotus Workplace allows for a new class of collaborative and organizational productivity applications to be built. This new modular component-based infrastructure will provide an environment where innovations can be created by business professionals. The tooling provided is designed for knowledge workers and business-oriented people to build on the new ways of interacting.

We also have to change the current collaboration paradigm, because e-mail systems worldwide are being overloaded. For example, people often keep all their documents or project management within their e-mail systems. E-mail changed the way people worked. Initially, companies did not use e-mail as a central collaborative system. In fact, initially some companies resisted e-mail deployments. Now, companies have built many core business processes around e-mail. E-mail is the first thing most people check when going into the office.

We have seen similar resistance and then contrasting emerging success to other collaborative user capabilities, such as instant messaging. Some company executives have told us, "We don't want instant messaging because people will only use it to chat about the weekend football game or exchange gossip." Interestingly, at many companies and organizations of all sizes, instant messaging systems have been deemed "mission critical." Some businesses have long implemented instant messaging and experienced significant productivity gains, cost savings, and reduction in use of e-mail. IBM's CFO office has deemed IBM's implementation of Lotus Sametime (Lotus Instant Messaging) to be a "mission-critical" application because it is used in many ways worldwide to securely communicate among IBM employees. Sametime has also become essential at the end of each year's quarter because people in 164 countries use secure instant messaging as a communications mechanism among the IBM finance people for the closing of the financial books.

As we moved from just doing personal productivity into the era of team productivity, we all had to think differently in order to have new visionary ideas of what could happen and then experience those new productive approaches. Similarly, as we now learn from and move from the era of team productivity into the era of business or organizational productivity, we have to think differently and envision the conceptual approaches, and then see those new visionary approaches turn into reality.

For example, let's consider all that is involved in planning a meeting and the fact that different people may have different ways of doing such, some better than others. Wouldn't it be good if we could capture the best way of planning a meeting, create a template, and share it? Right now, this could be done by creating a document that lists all that is involved, such as the to-do list, whom to contact, equipment ordering process, and catering options. But this overall process involves people and artifacts such as calendars, e-mails, chats, phone calls, forms, authorizations, payment processing, alerts for critical steps, or requirements. Having a document listing what to do requires people to read the document and follow each step. Maybe someone will not read all of the document, missing something important, like a footnote that says, "ensure the PC projector can project at high resolution," and they get the wrong projector. Maybe there are authorizations that need to take place, and a new person may not realize that these authorizations are essential or take two to three weeks to process, yet the meeting is next week. Using the traditional applications to manage this process can work, but it is not the ideal approach. Having a new approach and the technology for managing processes will enable such things as planning a meeting to be more effectively defined and integrated with all the relevant elements and people.

In this new era, we'll leverage the technologies and applications of personal productivity and team productivity. We will also leverage new technologies that enable us to define things such as an activity thread and all the elements that are associated with that activity.

Component-Based Services

The IBM Workplace architecture comprises many different services. As you have seen in this book, the goal of Lotus Workplace was to create an infrastructure for building collaborative applications. This was done by first creating a set of collaborative services that can be grouped together to form applications as required. Not only that, they could be used within custom applications as well to enhance the productivity of the end user for normal business processes. Template applications could be made on which users could build.

The rich client was developed to allow for a much richer user experience. Because the rich client environment is managed at the server, the cost of implementing the client is the same as implementing a typical Web browser. Yet, the rich function that is now possible with the rich client matches and exceeds that of any traditional desktop environment.

The applications delivered with Lotus Workplace (such as Lotus Workplace Messaging, Lotus Workplace Team Collaboration, Lotus Workplace Documents, and Lotus Workplace Collaborative Learning) are all applications that have a selected group of services combined to create those applications. However, the grouping of the services is arbitrary and was made because most users would be familiar with the applications provided. Lotus provided the base set of applications to help enable a fast start to implementation. But, consider the flexibility that now exists. In the past, if you liked the way most of an application environment, such as an e-mail and calendar system, worked, but did not like one or two aspects of it, you did not really have much choice but to accept it as one package. With Lotus Workplace, if you like the calendar application, but want to change how one of the scheduling components worked, you could build your own component.

New Ways to Build Applications

Because of the architecture of the Lotus Workplace product, we can rearrange the services to produce new ways of building collaborative applications. The rich client allows us to build a customized user interface to access the services. So, we can create an environment where new possibilities are available and endless. For example, we could embed awareness inside a business application such as a human resource application. The human resource application would be able to query a list of employees and if those employees were online then they would be indicated inside of the application. The end user could directly communicate with that employee through the chat mechanism. Another example might be to incorporate Team Space services into an application that shares customer information amongst a group of employees. In this example, an employee might click on a customer object that brings up the applicable menu that would allow them to create discussion threads specifically about that customer. Instead of having to go to a separate area for threaded discussions, it would be embedded into the fabric of the application.

Changing the Face of Collaboration

Another example of an application that can be built is included with the Lotus Workplace rich client. Activity Explorer is a rich client-based application that attempts to change the face of collaboration. It utilizes the services of the Lotus Workplace server and presents them to the user in a new way. Activity Explorer is not a separate product one needs to buy. Activity Explorer is a functional component that comes included within the rich client environment.

When we talk about collaborative applications, we usually think about mail, team rooms, Web conferencing, documents, and so on as distinct applications. In fact, in many day-to-day activities, we may use all of these applications to accomplish a single activity.

For example, responding to a RFP or closing a sale may involve sending mail or chatting with other members of a team to discuss a document in a repository or Team Space. Web conferences are also set up to get the group together to work on the content of the documents. A user must navigate to different applications in order to accomplish these tasks. Although this has made the user more productive, it could be improved.

Activity Explorer is a new component within Lotus Workplace that allows you to move to the concept of "instant collaboration," allowing you to capture ad hoc collaborative workflows around objects all within a single user interface. It tracks the elements of collaboration, links process threads, and keeps track of process threads by capturing them in motion.

There are three basic root elements of collaboration: people, shared objects (chat sessions, documents, etc.), and activities. We create a people element, which may be the profile information of person defined as an object. The shared objects already exist in various forms, such as e-mail, chat session content, documents, Web conference links, etc. As illustrated in Figure 4.1, the activities resemble connective tissues that grow as a process evolves. The evolution is bidirectional as the collaboration process becomes formalized.

For example, a few people may have a conversation that results in an idea someone thinks about. That idea is pondered, and maybe through other conversations with other people, the idea grows into a potential opportunity or project. Through further interactions, such as instant message chat sessions with a group of people, decision makers decide to formalize the idea into a formal task or project. Various elements may exist in the formation of this idea into a project, such as documents, Web site linkages, access to databases, and distribution lists of people involved. As the ad hoc collaboration develops and people are added to the collaboration, drag-and-drop actions are performed to pull people elements into the process thread, triggering automatic updates and access authority to the relevant shared objects.

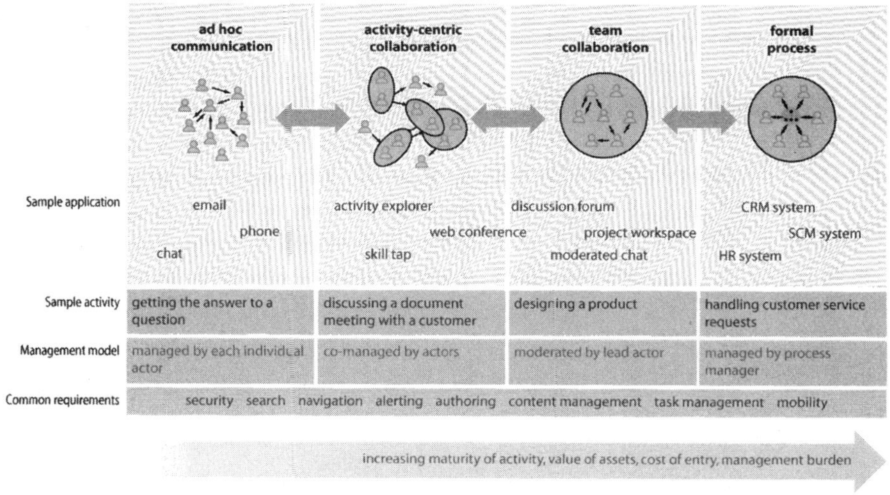

Figure 4.1. Activities evolve from adhoc communication to formal processes.

Let's take a look at another example of two people who need to discuss a document, such as a presentation for a customer. As seen in Figure 4.2, the main Activity Explorer view of the Lotus Workplace shows a list of activities that the user is participating in that is available. Selecting an activity will then list all the associated activity threads. In this example, to start the activity we can simply drag the presentation file from on our desktop and drop it on the name of the person we want to collaborate with in the contact list. This simple task has already invoked a number of Lotus Workplace services. When the presentation file was dropped on the user's name, the document was moved to a document repository on the server using the Lotus Workplace document services. Then, the member list was updated on the repository to allow access to the document, and finally the "inbox" service of the Lotus Workplace server was used to place a notification in the activity list of both users. Instead of navigating to these services through the standard user interface, they were accomplished with one simple action.

Now that the activity has been started and is available to both users, new artifacts can be added to the thread. For example, a new message could be

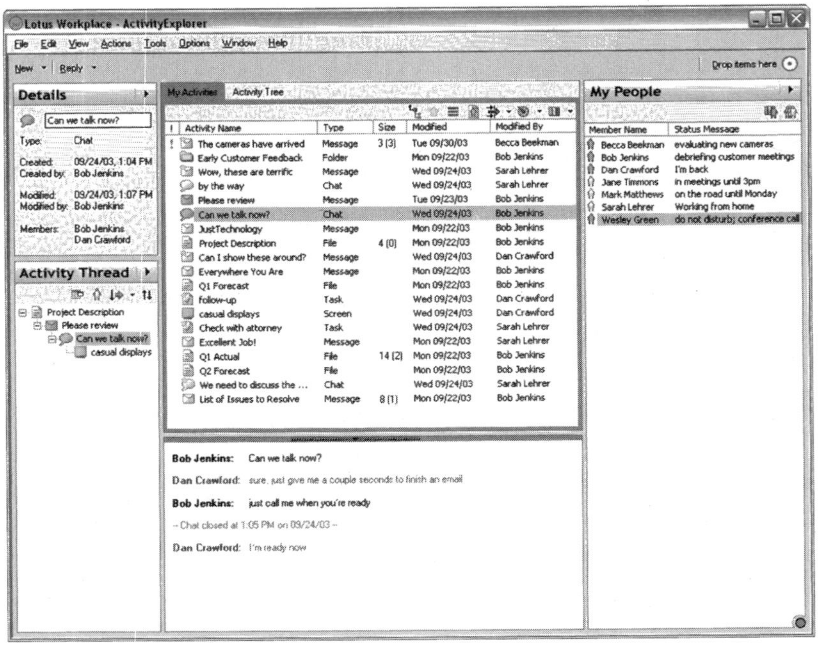

Figure 4.2. IBM Workplace Activity Explorer.

attached to the document as a way to communicate asynchronously with the other user. A chat could be started when the other person is online. These activities are attached to the thread. An ad hoc meeting that utilizes the screen-sharing service could also be added directly from this thread. As seen in Figure 4.2, users can invoke the collaborative services they need, just in time, within the same user interface. The users can easily see all the activities that have been associated with the tasks by simply clicking on the activity and seeing all the activities in a treelike view.

Since all of these activity threads are stored in the Lotus Workplace repository, they can be "mined" for knowledge. Best practices could be discovered for the ad hoc types of activities that people do every day and then could be templated inside the Lotus Workplace environment so that they can be shared throughout the enterprise. This could dramatically assist in training new employees.

Activity Explorer changes the way users interact with the system. Just as in the past with e-mail or instant messaging systems, we are sure that some people's first reaction will be resistance to this change. We are at the very beginning of the new wave of organizational productivity. It is early in the life of new application components such as Activity Explorer. It too will be updated and modified as user feedback is obtained.

Today, Activity Explorer is a sample application component that demonstrates the possibilities available with the Lotus Workplace architecture. Is it the "killer app" of this new generation of collaboration? We're not sure. But then again, we didn't know that a small sample application such as e-mail, which came included with Notes/Domino, would change the way organizations work today either! The Notes/Domino environment has over 100 million users. In fact, it is also the most widely used word processor in the world today. More e-mails and documents are created in Lotus Notes than any other rich text document editor. Componentization and commoditization of personal productivity applications, such as office editors, has enabled rich new functions for team productivity. Componentization and commoditization of both office editors and other team productivity applications will contribute to enabling new possibilities for organizational productivity. With these changes and new products, such as Lotus Workplace, we may not know the killer app yet, but we do know that it will appear.

5

Industry Solutions

This chapter discusses various industries and highlights some of the challenges they face that are addressed by various IBM industry solutions. We will refer to a few examples of the solutions available from IBM, but we won't list and name all the available solutions, as there are simply too many. Plus, there will be more solutions made available over the life of this book. Please refer to the IBM software Web site *www.ibm.com/software/solutions* for more details.

To become an On Demand Business™, IBM believes that there are two key imperatives that apply to all businesses across all industries (see Figure 5.1). As discussed in Chapter 1, the first imperative is "Innovating the business to differentiate and capture new value." The second imperative is, "Improving the productivity of resources deployed." To address these imperatives, the overall IBM software portfolio provides a complete and specialized portfolio of best-in-industry middleware to accelerate the execution of business strategy and the delivery of business value. The IBM Workplace family is a major part of the IBM software portfolio that delivers the necessary architectural foundation and a vast array of component services that will change the game of how application functions are provided to both traditional users and new user communities.

IBM software group is executing a strategy to deliver industry middleware solutions in a mix of ways driven by the market. Market research indicates that organizations and businesses find significant value in industry-specific middleware solutions, as they want to implement and move toward business-related projects. Key attributes that customers desire include demonstrable vendor experience in their industry implementing the solutions, support from

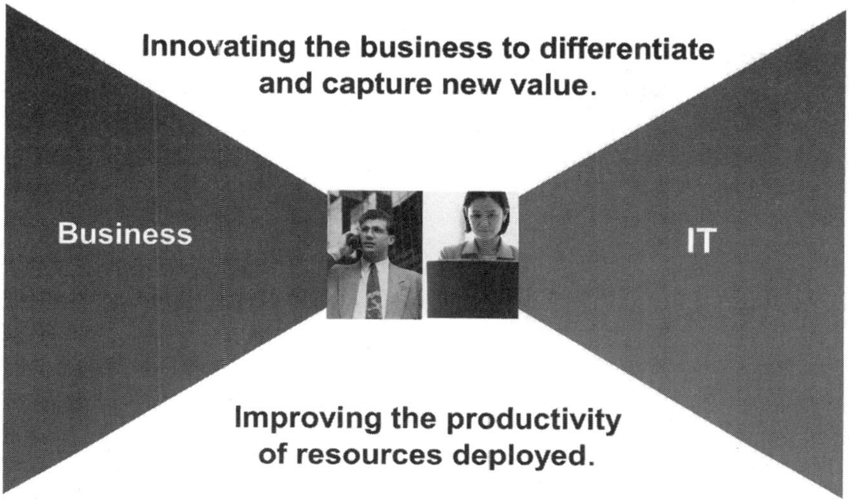

Figure 5.1. Imperatives in today's world.

independent software vendors and systems integrators prevalent in their industry and essential to their project, and the flexibility to address their unique business needs while providing a "head start" on the tasks associated with delivering integrated end-to-end solutions. IBM delivers industry middleware solutions, with proven industry experience, breadth of capabilities, and ability to promote unbiased relationships with independent software vendors (ISVs) and system integrators (SIs).

The industry middleware solutions that IBM is bringing to market leverage the skills and industry expertise of IBM's Software Sales team and Business Consulting Services (BCS) team. The IBM industry middleware solutions include capabilities from across IBM's five software brands combined with a strong partner ecosystem, in which BCS is a key player, to speed project implementation and to reduce risk. The IBM software group industry solutions team collaborated with BCS to select the top customer priorities in each industry, and worked with the software brands to create solutions to address these priorities. These solutions map to the IBM On Demand Operating Environment capabilities.

IBM delivers industry solutions through three different IBM organizations. The IBM Industry Sales team delivers industry-specific solutions that utilize these technologies and products. The BCS industry team delivers service-based solutions via the IBM On Demand Workplace, which provides WebSphere Portal-based solutions customized for specific industries. Organizations within IBM Software Group (for example, Lotus) are also producing product-based solutions that utilize the IBM Workplace technologies that are industry specific. Many solution offerings from IBM are available with a combination of IBM Software; IBM Services; business partner applications; and, when appropriate, hardware too.

IBM Workplace Solutions

There are many cross-industry *value-capturing* and *productivity* benefits that can be gained by using the IBM Workplace Family of products. Every industry has user communities that are usually ignored technologically because the cost of traditional computing implementations is too costly. With IBM Workplace, it is now affordable to provide nontraditional user communities with user functions such as Web-based e-mail, calendaring, document editing, team rooms, online education, Web conferencing, and collaboration awareness.

All industry organizations could benefit from having a better handle on skills management and job role-based tracking/mapping of employee skill development. The Lotus Workplace learning software with role-based mapping provides such. Whether providing an entry-level new hire a roadmap to learning what they need to know or guiding executive development for key management, the role-based educational mapping linked with online educational software provides good value and productivity.

Collaborative awareness functions within any organization can provide tremendous cost savings. For example, e-mail systems and the data/documents stored within such systems have become central to most business operations and communications. Along with this, there are two common problems that often burden the IT systems. Disk storage becomes enormous because many people use e-mail as a form of document storage. The Lotus Workplace family provides a solution that enables a shared documents repository, and search and workflow engines across applications simplify support of business processes and reduce the storage requirements because people don't have to keep documents in their local e-mail system.

E-mail communication, although a powerful way to communicate, is often slower and more costly compared with instant messaging systems. The Lotus Workplace family has awareness capabilities that enable faster and responsive communications between people, which can significantly reduce the volume of e-mails.

The IBM Workplace family enables a flexible choice of hardware, operating systems, and user access points and thus preserves existing investments. The easy integration of applications simplifies support of the environment, thereby reducing costs. The modular, on demand licensing (pricing) model accommodates seasonal fluctuations in staffing. Centrally managed application deployment and upgrades reduce IT workload. Dynamic provisioning of applications based on roles gives employees the right tools to maximize productivity and eliminates a costly one-size-fits-all approach. Built-in editors eliminate the need to provide everyone with the same complete (expensive) personal productivity tools. The standards-based portal simplifies integration of new and existing business applications.

As illustrated in Figure 5.2, the environment of the IBM Workplace solutions enables a productive and collaborative work environment by providing roles-based access to people, information, and processes. People within an organization's internal and external value chain can be equipped with the appropriate access to other people, processes, and information, from any device, based on the individual's role.

For a branch bank manager, a personalized user environment can be set up to deliver pertinent information about customers and employees at the branch level. The user's environment allows the branch manager to be connected to the other branches and to headquarters. The branch manager can have informa-

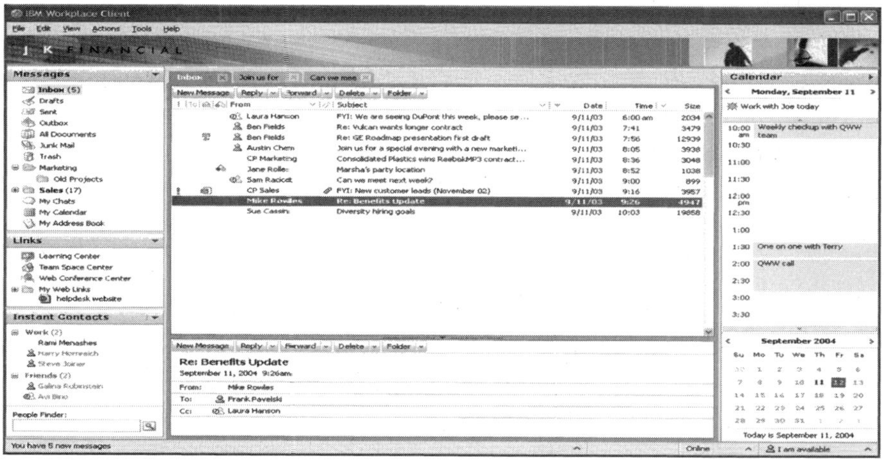

Figure 5.2. IBM Workplace rich client user environment.

tion to measure success and key performance indicators. Instead of searching widely for information, it is presented to the branch manager for analysis. IBM Workplace solutions masks the complexity of the underlying applications, data, networks, etc.

Because IBM Workplace solutions is based on a J2EE open standards middleware infrastructure that delivers standard file formats and a flexible architecture that accepts plug-ins, organizations have a single set of standards to manage. Flexible Workplace Client Technology offers enterprises a choice as to how to deploy solutions based on the way people work and the role they play in an organization. With rich client technology, a user can provision and manage data and applications from a server, work in "disconnected" mode, and reconnect/synchronize later. Other users may elect to have a browser-based Workplace because it is best suited to the way they work. Applications can be provisioned to PDAs and other pervasive devices to support mobile users.

IBM Workplace for Business Controls and Reporting

The need for compliance and risk management applies in all industries. Many businesses and organizations require an integrated, comprehensive compliance management solution. As discussed in Chapter 3, IBM Workplace for Business Controls and Reporting provides the knowledge and information management, portal, and collaboration infrastructure to help address internal business control and reporting requirements. This can provide top management with visibility into the effectiveness of a company's internal business controls. Document processes support the identification of risks and controls and facilitate the evaluation of the controls' effectiveness. Top executives can receive summaries and a compliance overview for their organization.

This solution helps provide a platform for an organization's business reporting process and an organized approach to gathering information about business controls, including controls over financial reporting. The environment can be customized to the role of the user. It provides an automated work flow to help document and evaluate internal business controls. Executive dashboards can allow management the ability to actively monitor the internal controls environment on a continuous real-time basis, thus helping management to assess the effectiveness of a company's internal business controls.

Document management, collaboration, training, and records management functions are all integrated with a single repository. The content repository forms the foundation for organizing control activities, disseminating information, and gathering the information required to help evaluate risk and monitor the internal control system. The knowledge-gathering and notification capabilities can help you to discover internal and external risks quickly so that you make timely and well-informed decisions.

This solution incorporates KPMG expertise, which helps leverage KPMG's industry insights and knowledge of internal control processes and practices. This is done using the KPMG Control Catalogs, available directly from KPMG at a separate charge.

The IBM Workplace for Business Controls and Reporting provides a foundation that will assist in an organization's efforts to assess its financial reporting in response to Section 404 of the Sarbanes-Oxley Act. This offering can help companies gather and monitor information about controls in a more consistent and organized manner. This Web-based, end-to-end solution can help provide users with greater visibility into a company's financial processes across the enterprise.

Aerospace and Defense

Aerospace and Defense (A&D) is an industry that strives for greater achievements and innovation. The defense industry is also undergoing major change, continuously restructuring its alliances and consolidating globally. These challenges place greater emphasis on the use of technology. Likewise for the aerospace industry, alliances, consolidation, and joint ventures are strategies for achieving greater cost advantages. As the imperatives of becoming an On Demand Business are applied to the A&D industries, there is a growing need for software to help people collaborate more effectively, to improve management of workflow, and to find cost-appropriate ways to bring nontraditional users into the realm of collaboration. To make the critical partnering and alliances a success, there must be good integration.

Companies are faced with an increasing requirement to make significant up-front investments; the payback period can be long and uncertain. The increased use of alliances, consortia, and subcontract arrangements are means of spreading the investment cost and risk across other companies. As illustrated in Figure 5.3, of IBM provides several solutions to address a variety of challenges faced by the A&D industry.

Aerospace and Defense companies often need to be able to play in a global marketplace. Alliances and joint ventures can help ensure that companies have a local presence to clinch the deal with customers and governments around the

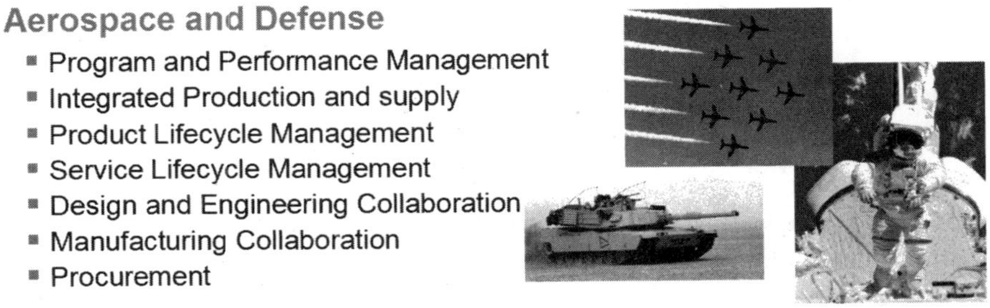

Figure 5.3. Aerospace and Defense industry solutions.

world. Companies need to balance these types of cooperation with their positioning in their own home countries in order to avoid losing national capability. In addition, contractors in the military sector often face demands from their customers for greater accountability in the use of public funds. Companies need to demonstrate their enhanced efficiency and productivity to a wide audience. Having reliable software solutions that can address the global needs while also supporting the local needs becomes critical.

Aerospace and defense is a global industry composed of designers, manufacturers, and servicers of military and commercial aircraft and ships, spacecraft, and related equipment. The A&D industry differs from most other commercial and consumer industries in a number of respects. Innovation in design focuses on safety, lifecycle cost effectiveness, passenger comfort, and speed. Airplanes and ships are manufactured in low volumes over long periods of time. This creates limited cost benefits from traditional economies of scale. The cost of overcoming technological barriers is usually high because the product research and development (R&D) effort is intense and constant. Aerospace and defense products must meet exacting performance standards and must operate in harsh physical environments. Aircraft operations, spacecraft launches, and battlefield hostilities are examples of such environments.

A common problem in the A&D manufacturing industry is the problem of inefficient collaboration. Using IBM Workplace solutions for A&D helps enable on demand manufacturing collaboration. For example, this could helps build an environment that would span data, process, human workflow, and business process optimization. And this can help with projects by creating user work environments facilitating a manufacturing portal and providing a process-based integration hub, a data warehouse, document/content management, a single sign-on and security infrastructure, business activity monitoring, and B2B integration with outsourced manufacturing.

A service-based offering called IBM On Demand Workplace for Aerospace and Defense is available from IBM's BCS division. IBM On Demand Workplace can help aerospace and defense companies reduce cycle times to start up new programs. An On Demand Workplace is designed to make it possible for employees, customers, suppliers, and partners to share information collectively. This solution is for managing large-scale defense and commercial programs efficiently as these are the lifeblood of the aerospace and defense industry. The ability to collaborate effectively is prerequisite to success, but bringing people, processes, data, and analysis together is a huge, global challenge. You can reduce cycle times and make better decisions in such a complex environment by aligning information, programs, people, and processes based on the role individuals play in your organization.

Automotive

With global market expansion, global vehicle sales continue to grow. But interestingly, manufacturers are challenged with the need to invest in new assembly facilities while the industry overall continues to be plagued by overcapacity. Automakers carry the burden of unnecessary capacity in both mature and emerging markets. With further investments going ahead around the globe, the conventional wisdom of capacity planning and balancing is being combined with new ways to deal with a persistent problem. The on demand imperatives of increasing productivity and capturing new value apply to the automotive industry. The need in the auto industry to do more partnering and alliances continues to increase.

Within the automotive industry, excess production capacity is driving major consolidation. This has created fierce pricing competition and vehicle sales fluctuations within the marketplace. Customers are demanding more vehicle variability, personalization, and value with quicker delivery. These changing market conditions, product pressures, and increased government regulation and reporting, such as for the Transportation Recall Enhancement Accountability and Documentation (TREAD) Act, introduced in 2000 in the United States, are putting tremendous pressure on eroding profit margins.

In North America, the automotive industry dynamics have gone through a fundamental change since the late 1990s. The result is a situation where there is little or no margin for error. At the same time, there is a growing requirement for partnering and leveraging OEMs to increase in order to improve their position in an ultra competitive marketplace. From new products and innovative technologies to flexible manufacturing and global expansion, OEMs are being pulled in several different directions at once. This places a large emphasis on the need for appropriate techniques to assist companies in the area of business planning and business productivity.

The European auto market is fragmented; however, with this fragmentation, in combination with a mass of other new product launches, there is opportunity to capture new value and stimulate a market increase. In China and other Asian countries, there is a strong demand for automobiles. In South America, they have had challenging times in terms of automobile demand, but there is the future to prepare for.

The challenge for most in the auto industry is not so much the current state of the market, but instead being able to quickly adapt to the changes that take place over time. Business flexibility is key to success in this kind of environment. Individual firms must be innovative and increase productivity in order to prosper amid a landscape littered with new competition, underutilized capacity, and massive overinvestment. The companies that are prepared to navigate its transforming competitive landscape will reap great rewards.

Tools such as alternative scenario forecasting are now available to help plan for, and adapt to, ever-changing market conditions. Due to the success of quarterly forecasting and automotive analysis, executives can make better decisions. Collaboration solutions to help pull the information together and assist the many people involved to provide the necessary and timely information to the executives are necessary. The breadth of people now participating in such a process and business productivity areas is dramatically increasing.

The automotive industry also has a significant number of employees that are nontraditional users of computer systems and office productivity applications. And the time is long overdue that these employees now be brought into the realm of computing, so they too can become more productive, participate in a variety of business processes, take online education, have access to corporate news and e-mail, and receive electronic pay stubs.

Manufacturers are searching for new sources of revenue while continuing to reduce operating costs. Rapidly changing profit zones put a high focus on initiatives to bring competitive design quickly to market, improving supply chain execution, reducing manufacturing costs, and enhancing marketing and branding management capabilities. These initiatives intrinsically require extensively integrated business processes to facilitate collaboration and information integration across the value chain. Manufacturers must strengthen their underlying business integration technologies to support initiatives to remain competitive, improve margins, and increase customer loyalty.

An automobile manufacturer of sedans, sports utility vehicles (SUVs), and luxury sports cars has a dealer network of storefront sales and service centers around the globe. To ensure optimum customer service and satisfaction while also increasing revenue and decreasing costs, it must keep its dealers up-to-date in several key areas: new product announcements, current and planned inventories, impending deliveries, promotions and specials, financing and leasing, and parts and service bulletins (including recalls).

IBM provides several solutions (see Figure 5.4) to address a variety of challenges faced by the Automotive industry. Managing relationships between manufacturer, dealers, and customers is difficult. Dealer-to-dealer communications is limited to phone and e-mail exchanges, resulting in delayed or missed customer opportunities. The manufacturer as well as its dealers frequently manage and stock an excessive inventory of automobiles as well as aftermarket parts, which may not align with customer demand. Dealers often aren't able to maintain one-to-one relationships with their customer base, which detracts from potential parts and service revenue as well as future sales of new and replacement vehicles.

Inefficient manual processes cut into revenues and add to costs. Information dissemination from the manufacturer to the dealer network is paper-based, cumbersome, and varied among dealers. This is time-consuming, costly, and adversely affects both the manufacturer's and dealers' bottom lines. Financing and leasing vehicles produces an additional revenue stream for many dealers. However, they must rely on an inconvenient paper-based system for qualifying and lending to customers. As a result, customers may seek other financing options, which can take a business day or more to close as well as depriving the

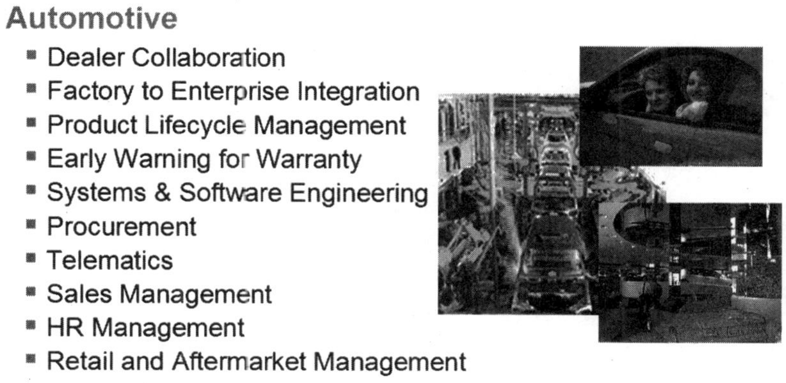

Figure 5.4. Automotive industry solutions.

dealer of this revenue source. Running promotions and specials mitigates the risks of overstocking and helps dealers be more competitive by giving customers a reason to buy. But slow or spotty communication of the details from the manufacturer to the dealers undercuts potential sales.

Enabled by IBM Workplace Client Technology, solutions available from IBM will help users access/interact with a single e-mail/calendar system and optionally take mail/calendar with them in a mobile environment. They will be able to securely communicate in real time with colleagues and dealers in the network. Using built-in editors, they can quickly run numbers for would-be car owners. Within the user environment, they can maintain a single point of access, based on their individual role or job, to all tools and applications, and can receive alerts (not faxes or snail mail) when there is a new promotion, special offer, or even a manufacturer's recall. This helps to automate processes, creating a consistent customer experience of buying and owning an automobile. It will increase the sales of services, parts, and replacement vehicles by better establishing one-to-one relationships with customers. This provides personalized delivery of operational, marketing, and critical product information to dealers. Personnel in the parts department can quickly locate critical parts so that the customers can be up-and-running ASAP and the personnel can better manage massive inventory and dealer overstocking.

The Automotive Dealer Collaboration solution addresses the challenges associated with managing aftermarket partners, massive inventory and overstocking, and manual and inefficient processes. This product provides an integrated architecture for extended enterprise collaboration that extends back-office systems directly to channel partners and dealers. This solution can be used for projects such as B2B/channel integration, Enterprise Resource Planning (ERP) integration, supply-chain Web Services, dealer portals, single sign-on/secure access, and mobile/pervasive device connectivity.

The Product Lifecycle Management solution addresses the problem of having disconnected teams and processes in the product development lifecycle by providing an integrated platform and application suite for improved collaboration to simplify the IT environment to support PLM, enhance product innovation, and lower costs. This business infrastructure, development, integration, and collaboration platform for the auto industry can be used in projects such as business process integration, B2B integration, supplier portals, product manager workplace, digital media asset management, workflow, and single sign-on/secure access.

The Factory to Enterprise Integration solution addresses the problem of ineffective communication/integration between factory floor data and the enterprise applications. This comprehensive architecture for integrating people, processes, and information can help improve operational performance, improve asset utilization, and provide real-time monitoring of production status. It is designed for use in projects such as ERP integration, portals, a data warehouse for analyzing factory data, single sign-on/secure access, digital asset management, a document/content management repository, and B2B supplier integration.

The Automotive Early Warning for Warranty solution addresses the challenges faced due to lack of visibility into early warranty systems. This solution enables an analytics and collaboration platform that automates early warning processes and enables TREAD Act reporting. This solution can be used in projects such as data warehouse analytics, portals, workflow, and business integration, and in enabling a collaborative workplace.

The Automotive Systems and Software Engineering solution addresses the complexity in the software engineering process. This solution provides a structured and integrated set of development tools and methodologies that propels improved software quality, accelerated development, and lower costs. This comprehensive, unified platform for development, testing, and deployment can assist automotive companies with development projects. It can be used in projects such as enabling a supplier portal, enabling a customer portal, facilitating B2B integration, community/marketplace integration, data warehousing/analytics, process-based business integration, plant-to-SAP integration, and single sign-on with secure access.

The Telematics solution enables the connection to provide interactive communication to vehicles and perform remote diagnostics, prognostics, and software updates. By gaining insight into vehicle performance, it reduces warranty costs. It can assist with directions and dynamically route vehicles based on demand volumes, traffic, or road conditions. This can monitor and manage driver safety, fuel consumption, cargo lifecycle, and vehicle health.

The IBM Telematics solution has helped many automobile companies implement the OnStar system and improves the accuracy of their hands-free voice recognition capabilities and in delivering voice enhancement capability through a user's wireless phone that works inside and outside the vehicle.

Banking and Financial Markets

The banking and financial markets industries are undergoing tremendous change, driven by growing management acceptance that Internet-driven business and Internet-based commerce are real and will be vital differentiating factors for future survival and competitiveness. The change to a network economy is occurring faster than most people expected. The banking and financial markets industries are made up of firms that offer a wide range of financial services. Generally, these industries include retail banking, corporate banking, wholesale (commercial) banking, and financial markets.

The banking industry, which has existed for centuries and is known for its traditions of conservatism and dependability, is now facing tremendous changes, including deregulation, pressures on profit margins, globalization, and intensified competition from traditional and nontraditional providers of financial services. In addition, a flurry of merger activity is creating megabanks, each hoping to offer a broad range of products and services and to leverage economies of scale.

The Internet has brought about a revolution that is real, and changes in the network economy are occurring faster than most people expected. Exponential growth is expected in every segment of the online financial services industry. The emerging network economy is challenging all financial institutions to understand, develop strategies for, and invest in business. This challenge requires new business models and new ways of approaching relationships with customers.

As illustrated in Figure 5.5, IBM provides several Banking and Financial Market industry solutions. Banking and financial market companies are experiencing significant changes in behavior and expectations in their customer sets as a result of the movement toward a network-based economy. The networked world, which provides instant access to customers and competitors, is disrupting traditional business models. These models were geographically focused,

Figure 5.5. Banking and Financial Markets industry solutions.

product oriented, and based on controlled growth strategies. Changes include such things as regulatory and legislative change, mergers and acquisitions; new-entrant activity; market demand; macroeconomic restructuring; credit; market risk concentration; technology revolution; and rigorous cost management.

As illustrated in Figure 5.6, with IBM Workplace solutions, financial staff can be provided with a role-based user experience, each customized with a view of and access to the applications and functions they need to do their job. These solutions can provide common calendar and scheduling functions that would enable users to exchange meeting invitations with employees across the company regardless of mail platform. Collaborative applications deployed via intranet would increase the effectiveness of business resources (people, teams, applications, and content) across geographically dispersed divisions. Communication between employees across locations and business units can be drastically improved with instant messaging. Employees can locate colleagues and experts faster with People Finder and an enterprise-wide directory. An integrated family of collaborative products provides individuals and teams with faster access to the right information and people to maximize business productivity. Secure document management and auditable (virtual) paper trails improve the ability to manage enterprise risk. Providing employees with a common experience across all products and applications (for example, teaming, learning, and messaging), although their purposes are different, makes it easier to train and reduces training overhead.

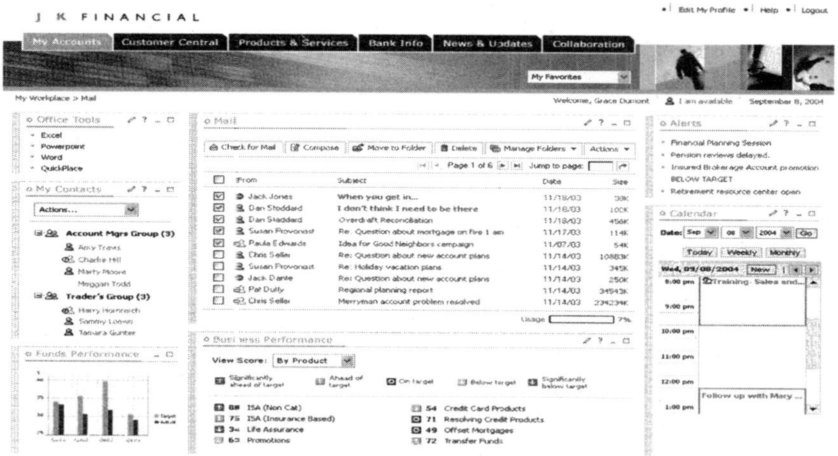

Figure 5.6. IBM Workplace browser-based user environment.

The Banking Core Systems Transformation solution addresses the challenges faced when modernizing, transforming, integrating, migrating, and consolidating core banking systems. This process-driven, business infrastructure enables faster roll-out of new products and channels, and provides a consolidated view of the customer banking employees. This IBM solution provides unique capabilities to extend traditional banking platforms to the Web. This solution can be used in projects in which a business wants to provide core banking Web services, an online portal, business process modeling and optimization, a customer data warehouse, a security management infrastructure, Web application development, or CRM integration.

The Wholesale Payments Processing solution looks at the problem of having fragmented payments systems, as well as other new networks, such as SWIFTNet. It works to integrate payments messaging architecture with SWIFT support, which will in turn lower transaction costs and improve visibility and monitoring. Projects such as SWIFTNet migration, automated payment director, payment security, process integration hub, and financial network messaging consolidation will benefit from this solution.

Enabling a twenty-first-century branch IT infrastructure is a problem many banks encounter. The Branch Transformation solution addresses this challenge. Using an integrated, consolidated architecture for each bank branch can lower operational costs and improve the overall management of the branch. This end-to-end solution is for modernizing and transforming branch IT infrastructure. Projects using this solution include branch teller portals; branch self-service and kiosk applications; remote, centralized management infrastructure; branch employee work environment; a customer data warehouse and analytics; and wireless mobile banking.

The Channel Empowerment solution addresses the problem of inconsistent customer treatment based on different channels. This uses an integrated architecture for customer data, customer relationship management, and customer information management applications. It allows banks to have multichannel service, automated personalized interactions, and campaigns. This solution can be used in projects such as implementing pervasive or mobile devices, voice response applications, online customer service, transactional applications, customer data warehouses, and contact center/CRM integration.

Banks and financial institutions deal daily with regulatory compliance such as Basel II, Sarbanes-Oxley, and the U.S. Patriot Act. The risk and compliance management solution offers a comprehensive infrastructure for managing people, processes, and information related to business controls and regulatory compliance. It enables banks to speed up their time to compliance as well as lower costs. This solution delivers the advanced information infrastructure required to address the evolving economic, regulatory, and shareholder issues facing financial markets firms today. This solution is tailored toward projects and leverages products such as Workplace for Business Controls and Reporting. This helps provide process-based integration hubs, data warehouses, document/content management, single sign-on and security infrastructures, data mining and specialized analytics (fraud detection), and business activity monitoring.

The Financial Markets Trade and Order Management solution addresses the problem of enabling automated real-time trading. It enables automated, event-driven trading and analytics to help capital markets firms exploit arbitrage opportunities, eliminate the trade-off between speed and robustness, and offer sophisticated tools to institutional customers. The Financial Markets Trade and Order Management solution leverages computing, database, and business-activity monitoring technologies to enable true real-time data retrieval and high-performance analysis of large quantities of real-time and historical time-stamped data.

The Financial Markets Front Office Insight solution helps in presenting an integrated product portfolio to institutional clients. This solution is designed to deliver integrated front-office services to help financial firms increase sales productivity, enable frictionless knowledge sharing, and extract full value from research. The IBM solution allows firms to enhance the provision of products and services to their customers using an interface capable of aggregating customer, product, and market data. Its capabilities help firms to better understand customer needs through aggregation of positions across independent lines of business and to pursue sophisticated trading and wealth-management strategies.

The Financial Markets Financial Information Interchange solution addresses the problems faced when managing connectivity to multiple financial networks and exchanges. This solution is designed to help financial firms manage critical business processes that span enterprise boundaries, allowing them to outsource non-core functions, leverage industry utilities, and offer seamless connectivity to partners. The solution delivers capabilities required for firms to connect their customers to market infrastructures. Whether the infrastructure is an exchange, an industry utility, or an outsourced service provider, the IBM Middleware Solution for Financial Markets Financial Information Interchange offers firms the capabilities to integrate information and manage business process results, regardless of where the data is located or the processes are executed.

The Financial Markets Post-Execution Integration solution addresses the problem of trade failure rates. Such failures are also expensive and often involve manual processing. This solution delivers the capabilities for integrating the people, processes, and data involved in the business processes that happen after a trade is executed on an exchange. Using IBM and partner software, this solution enables firms to reduce the costs of trade processing through the elimination of reference data problems, automation of manual repair processes, and integration of front-, middle-, and back-office business processes. Increased straight-through processing rates, coupled with a reduction in failed trades and operational costs, translate to higher efficiency and improved customer service.

IBM Workplace for Branch Banking

IBM Workplace for Branch Banking solution is built using the IBM Workplace products and technologies. This solution can help retail banks increase sales, improve customer services and enhance the productivity of their customer-facing employees. This solution provides role-specific environments for branch managers, tellers and platform officers.

Consumer Products

In the consumer products industry, the focus is on leveraging brands and uncovering new distribution channels to drive revenue, as well as cost reductions through industry-cooperative initiatives. Industry consolidation is expected to continue, with more corporate mergers as well as continued selling and acquiring of major brands. Recently, the top 80 consumer products companies in the United States and Europe have joined forces to create a powerful B2B trading exchange called *Transora*.

As illustrated in Figure 5.7, IBM provides several solutions to address the needs of the Consumer Products industry. There is a lot of competition and tight margins in the consumer products industry. Lack of top-line revenue growth

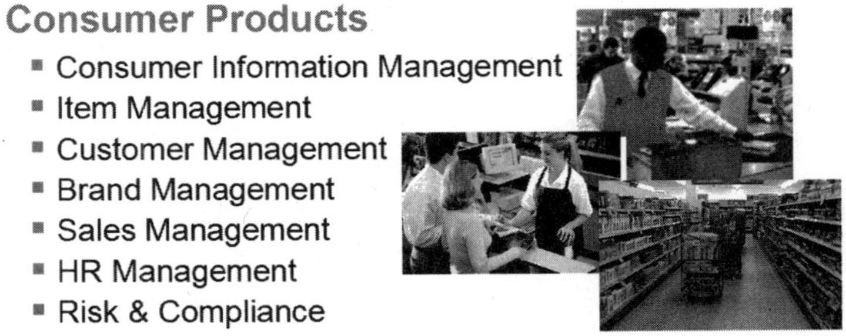

Figure 5.7. Consumer Products industry solutions.

continues to plague the industry. The ability to react quickly to market demands has been hampered by a complex organizational structure. Consumer products processes span marketing and sales, manufacturing, procurement and distribution, research and development, human resources, and IT.

Item maintenance inaccuracies, invoice billing errors, and lag time are all problems addressed by the Item Management solution. It offers a comprehensive next-generation architecture for UCCNet item management, radio frequency identification or RFID (a generic term for technologies that use radio waves to automatically identify people or objects) architecture, and B2B integration. This allows for faster and lower-cost delivery and integration of product information into the retail demand chain as well as increased visibility of the information. This solution is designed for projects such as UCCNet connectivity, business integration hubs, ERP integration, trading partner collaboration, retailer/customer management workplaces, and inventory management.

The Customer Management solution addresses the problem of sales force inefficiency due to administrative tasks and the lack of best practice sharing. This solution is an integrated architecture that enables the integration of people, processes, and information, as well as the delivery of up-to-date product, marketing, and inventory information to the sales force. Using the Customer Management solution results in higher productivity, enhanced planning and collaboration, and reduced manual and administrative time. This solution can be used in projects such as sales portals, customer management workplaces, trading partner collaboration, ERP integration, Customer Relationship Management (CRM) integration, and single sign-on/secure access.

Lack of control in content creation and workflow can be a problem, as can duplicating copies per medium and the difficulty with managing consistency across multiple channels. The Brand Management solution integrates a digital media repository with common portal front-end access, which improves quality control and streamlines version control. Projects that use this solution include digital media asset management, brand content portals, single sign-on secure access, data integration of heterogeneous content repositories, and workflow for version control of assets.

When there is a lack of integration between retail point of sale (POS) data and manufacturing information, the Consumer Information Management solution is able to help. It provides real-time integration across a supply chain and multiple POS systems. This leads to improved category management through the ability to deliver category management data to retailers faster. Projects that would utilize this solution include ERP integration, retailer B2B integration (trading partner collaboration), customer information portals, and business process modeling and workflow management.

The Risk and Compliance Management solution addresses the problem of compliance with regulations and filing deadlines as well as consolidating information from multiple units and the lack of documentation of business processes and controls. It has an integrated architecture for managing people, processes, and information, which leads to a faster response to reporting regulations, identifying key issues, and retaining the history. This solution can be used in projects such as risk and compliance workplaces, portals, business intelligence, data warehouses for financial reporting, and business process integration.

IBM Workplace for Consumer Products Customer Management

IBM Workplace for Consumer Products Customer Management provides the ability to access information from legacy systems and drive additional sales revenue, thereby improving bottom line results through fact-based decision making, collaboration, and communication. Sales employees can master new product sets through timely and effective e-learning at the point of need. Sales managers leverage online portal access to real-time pricing data, inventory levels, and promotional and buying trends.

Account managers can see key performance indicators quickly and understand sales trends, brand sales, and adjust to meet business conditions in real time. Productivity can increase by streamlining all nonsales and sales activities with focus on value-added activities. This also assists to reduce training costs while making individuals more effective, thus filling skills and knowledge gaps.

Sales information can be dispersed, redundant, and unreliable. Trade fund campaigns are highly manual in nature and over 60 percent of campaigns are unprofitable. IBM Workplace for Consumer Products Customer Management provides the ability to access information from legacy systems and drive additional sales revenue, thereby improving bottom line results through fact-based decision making, collaboration, and communication.

Electronics

A consumer electronics retail chain, with hundreds of outlets throughout a country, strives to provide the products customers want at the best price possible. Special promotions are often communicated weekly, and results are reported from outlets to headquarters. Inventory levels are closely monitored and managed and must be accessible to all employees. Online customers must have access to the same inventory system to ensure order fulfillment. District managers, who often take work home or on the road, are critical information brokers to both headquarters and the stores, and they must also have a view into the timely information they need. As companies in the electronics industry work to become on demand businesses, there are many new requirements that must be addressed.

The electronics industry is experiencing rapid change, primarily because of what is known as 3C convergence: the merging of computers, consumers, and communications. An example of this 3C convergence is the additional functionality you expect when you buy almost any consumer electronics product today, with both software and electronics embedded (pervasive computing).

The growth expectation of the electronics industry, fueled by the explosion in Internet capabilities, is greater than in any other industrial sector. The key challenges to the success of electronics firms in various industry segments and around the world involve issues such as customer satisfaction, time to market, innovation, and cost reduction.

The Internet is playing a major role in driving change and helping companies achieve their business goals. The use of the Internet solutions for competitive advantage has also caught the attention of CEOs in the electronics industry. Their goal is to use Internet-based technology to improve their internal processes and to enhance their external relationships with suppliers, distributors, and customers.

As illustrated in Figure 5.8, IBM provides several solutions to address the needs of the Electronics industry. With IBM Workplace solutions, communications among employees, managers, and headquarters is drastically improved with instant messaging, notifications sent for urgent items, and people finder. Managers can collaborate on employee issues and ideas, and coordinate quar-

Figure 5.8. Electronics industry solutions.

terly forecasting, etc. Employees can access corporate notifications, corporate calendars for special events, and receive electronic pay stubs. It will be easier for managers to assign and track daily employee activities; schedule group training events; and track holidays, vacation, and work schedules. Managers can maintain access to critical business communications even when traveling or unconnected from the corporate network using the offline capabilities.

Employee training through online self-paced courses would help keep the workforce well trained despite high turnover, which is common in the electronics industry. Employees can find information faster by having a single location containing company and personal information, including company notices, employee benefits, performance versus plans, district view for forecasting and planning, corporate view with aggregated business performance data/modeling, and inventory tracking, allowing them to work more efficiently.

Centrally managed application deployment and upgrades eliminate the need to touch every desktop, reducing IT workload and ensuring that all users are on latest versions of software. Dynamic provisioning of applications is policy based as determined by individual roles and needs, eliminating costly "one-size-fits-all" approaches and giving employees the right tools to maximize productivity.

To help manage IT costs better, standards-based capabilities let you leverage the existing infrastructure, thus preserving your prior investments. Having a flexible choice of hardware, operating systems, and user access points together with ease of integration simplifies support of the environment, reducing costs. The on demand licensing model accommodates seasonal fluctuations in staffing, lowering costs. The built-in editors are sufficient for many users, eliminating the need to provide everyone with the same complete (expensive) personal productivity suites.

The Electronics Product Innovation Management solution provides a collaborative engineering environment for the electronics manufacturer and addresses the problem of ineffective outsourcing and design processes and systems. The solution synchronizes outsourced product design data with internal engineering systems and enables collaboration across engineering groups using virtual design models. Key benefits are shortened development cycle time, increased design productivity and quality, and the ability to leverage outsourced design models.

The Electronics Software Lifecycle Management solution is designed to help electronics organizations meet the challenge of complex system design. The solution provides the software platform, software development tools, and embedded software serviceability capability, combined with consulting and development services. The benefits of this solution are an improved software development process, reduced costs, improved quality, reduced cycle time, change management, and quick response to provide new/enhanced software function.

The Electronics Supply Chain Collaboration solution addresses the concern that many electronics firms have hundreds of disconnected partners in their supply chain. This solution can assist electronics organizations in their efforts to manage complex global supply chains. It allows reconciliation of demand, supply, and inventory, and the alignment of financial responsibilities with the supply agreement. It helps to standardize supplier and customer process interactions to speed execution and information sharing. The benefits of this solution are adherence to industry standards such as RosettaNet, reduced operational response times, and increased visibility throughout the partner community.

The Electronics Business Performance Management solution addresses the problems faced by organizations that have poor information and visibility into business-level metrics for reporting, are challenged by regulatory compliance, and want more agility in rapidly changing markets. This solution provides capabilities for proactive management and quick response to rapidly changing customer demands and partner capabilities. It provides monitored information in the context of key performance indicators to help detect and analyze critical business conditions and respond the moment the conditions arise. This can result in improved decision making to optimize business results. Key benefits are minimized perishable inventory, real-time demand planning, a higher finished goods turn rate, lower overall inventory carrying costs, and elevated order replenishment ratings. This solution can be used for projects such as building a workplace for business controls, security access and identity controls, providing an integrated directory, document management, business integration between key applications, process modeling and monitoring, and workflow management.

The Electronics Risk and Compliance solution helps address the challenges of meeting regulatory compliance (e.g., Sarbanes-Oxley). This solution delivers capabilities to assist electronics organizations in their efforts to address management of internal controls requirements of the Sarbanes-Oxley Act. The solution provides integration of customer data and views of internal processes to support efforts to comply with multiple regulatory requirements.

Energy and Utilities

The global energy and utilities industry is more exposed than ever before to economic uncertainty and other problems. In a complex energy market, many companies are seeking to avoid risk by focusing on a clear point in the value chain. Some are choosing to diversify through multiproduct offerings, whereas others are refocusing their attention toward horizontal product and service differentiation. For all, the challenge will be to deliver a market model that offers incentives for investment, customer demand, market development, reduced costs, and competitive prices.

Virtually every government, business, and individual household is a customer of the utility and energy services industry. Products and services provided by companies in the industry traditionally include electricity, gas, water, and waste removal services.

To provide these products and services, utility companies own and operate a very often complex and geographically dispersed infrastructure, including generating stations, pumping stations, pipes, wires, meters, water treatment facilities, service fleets, and information technology systems.

While customers often take for granted the electricity that provides light, the gas that provides heat, and the water used for washing, they do have certain expectations of the utility companies that provide these things, such as a safe, reliable, adequate, and reasonably priced supply, easy-to-understand billing, and good customer service.

As illustrated in Figure 5.9, IBM provides several solutions to address the needs of the Energy and Utilities industry. Because utilities must deal with large (industrial), medium (commercial), and small (residential) customers, they must be able to provide a wide range of billing services, from the simple to the complex. In addition to having to meet customer expectations, the industry is dealing with fundamental changes in the way business is done. The primary fundamental change is that customers can now choose from whom they buy their energy services. Also, commodity trading of electricity and gas has emerged as a recent specialty segment of the industry. For example, some companies now buy electricity wholesale from a company that generates it and sells it retail to companies that distribute it to end-user customers.

Figure 5.9. Energy and Utilities industry solutions.

The Energy and Utilities Regulatory Compliance solution addresses the problems of new security regulations (e.g., Sarbanes-Oxley) and the increasingly complex risks of theft, corruption, destruction, and terrorism. The Regulatory Compliance solution addresses this by providing a comprehensive security policy infrastructure with business controls management to enable faster reporting and problem troubleshooting, as well as compliance with regulatory and government controls, including Sarbanes-Oxley. Projects that could utilize the Regulatory Compliance solution include building a workplace for business controls, security access and identity controls, an integrated directory, document management, business integration between key applications, process modeling and monitoring, and workflow management.

The Energy and Utilities Asset Operations solution addresses the problem of outage management time. Many companies want to reduce this, which can be done by using the Asset Operations solution. This integrated architecture enables real-time data accessibility, collaborative workflow and communication, and remote asset monitory to improve asset utilization and lower costs. This solution can be used by those involved in projects such as mobile employee connectivity/pervasive technologies, business integration between asset management systems and ERP, workflow for maintenance procedures, outage management portals, and outage application integration.

The Energy and Utilities Mobile Workforce Management solution looks at the problem of improving customer service while reducing the cost of services. This middleware supports field staff accessing corporate systems, from any device over any network, to improve response and resolution times and lower operations costs. Because this is an end-to-end secure solution, it enables customers to build flexible systems that are cost effective. Projects that can make use of this solution include computer-aided dispatch systems, credit and collections, inspections, outage management, work and asset management, gas leak management, and turning the meter on and off as well as reading it.

Often in the energy and utilities field there is a problem of having individual trading silos with a lack of responsiveness and flexibility. The Trading and Settlement solution is built on a comprehensive architecture that spans trading desks and distributes market data. The backbone to many trading floors is already MQ, which aids in the integration of this solution. It lowers operational costs and improves trading outcomes. Projects such as building a market-data messaging infrastructure, trading hub portals, institutional trader collaboration, trading system modernization, trading security and availability, time series analytics, trade master data management, and Sarbanes-Oxley compliance all benefit from this solution.

The Contact Center solution deals with customer and employee churn as well as the lack of integrated customer support operations. This solution improves response and resolution times, and lowers operational costs. Projects that could leverage this solution include document and content management, portals for customers, self-service, customer operations manager workplaces/portals, improved interactive voice response (IVR) or voice services, a single customer view across diverse customer information systems, customer analytics and profiling, customer information system (CIS) integration to other energy and utility systems, and building a commerce application Web site.

Government

Governments around the world undertake a range of common activities. The business and administrative challenges they face to improve the delivery of public services are also similar. These issues are driven by democratic pressure for increased transparency and accountability in government, consumer pressure for improved delivery of public services, and cost pressure to provide more and better infrastructure and services, more efficiently.

As illustrated in Figure 5.10, IBM provides several solutions to address the needs of Government and Government supporting organizations. Demands on governments are increasingly complex due to globalization of economies, citizen demands, and fiscal concerns. The industry focuses on e-government, revenue and fiscal management, postal and social services, and public safety and justice.

The Government Access solution addresses the problem of enabling citizen and business access to government information and services. This solution delivers versatile, end-to-end electronic business products and services to help provide citizens and businesses with one-stop, streamlined access to lo-

Figure 5.10. Government industry solutions.

cal, regional, and national government. It is designed to support multiple levels of government by providing constituents with convenient 24/7, user-friendly access to information, services, and benefits. It also offers collaboration tools to support government service representatives with complex online transactions. Key benefits are improved citizen and business access to information and services, increased government responsiveness, and a reduced burden of regulatory compliance for businesses. This solution provides a consolidated portal to provide Web-based access, which enables self-service and reduces administrative costs. It can be used in projects requiring business integration to streamline internal processes before exposing them to the public, in government Web services, in managing workflow, and in document management/content management.

The On Demand Government Workplace solution addresses the problem of reduced productivity of government employees due to paper-intensive and manual processes. This solution enables government employees to deliver higher value and increased productivity by efficiently finding and sharing information as they provide important services to constituents and businesses. The solution provides simplified access to personalized content and applications using role-based views, performance data, and just-in-time training and collaboration with experts. Key benefits are improved speed and quality of responses to routine and unexpected events, increased productivity, better cost management, and improved morale through employee self-service.

The Government e-Forms and Records Management solution addresses the problem of having costly, paper-based processes. This solution allows government employees to control document management and access, manage document retention, and reduce paper-based processes and redundant data entry. The records management component of the solution works within a content management infrastructure to provide formal, rules-based management for the processing, retention, and disposition of records. The e-Forms component allows government employees to complete, review, verify, route, and approve all forms securely and electronically using an intranet or extranet. Benefits are increased speed and quality of responses to information requests, reduced operating costs, and improved information integrity, retention, and security to manage compliance with regulations and standards.

The Government Collaboration solution addresses the problem of inefficient data and communication linkages between agencies. This solution provides an enterprise architecture to leverage existing systems and integrate processes that span government entities. It creates an environment for secure, real-time collaboration and knowledge sharing for governments and government departments to share applications and information, efficiently process information and requests, and interact with each other and with the private sector. By improving the information and technology infrastructure, this solution can greatly enhance the collaborating entities' efficiency while maintaining data security and privacy. Key benefits of the modernized enterprise architecture are higher-integrity multi-department processes, new and improved services to constituents, reduced operating costs, and improved cross-government decision making, coordination, and response to events.

The Government Emergency Response solution addresses the problem of having disparate sources of critical data impede emergency field operations. This solution enables emergency responders to have integrated access to a variety of spatial and attribute data across geopolitical boundaries to facilitate better and faster decision making. The solution provides seamless and secure integration of scattered and heterogeneous data through the use of federation, and enables more rigorous analysis and resource allocation through spatial visualization. The result is a complete view of timely information, anytime, anywhere, from across government and private organizations that can be leveraged in response to emergency situations. Key benefits are increased speed of response and access to integrated information, improved decision making, and improved, secure links among responding organizations.

Healthcare

Healthcare providers aim to improve the health and well-being of people. Patients often visit different clinics so current medical records are not always available at the point of care. Paper-based systems are disorganized and inconsistent, creating office inefficiency and inaccuracies resulting in lower patient satisfaction. Electronic medical record formats differ from clinic to clinic and are not easily integrated into a single patient record. Additionally, healthcare providers have a mobile workforce of doctors, nurses, and administrators who travel to various hospitals and clinics. Administrative reporting is complex and labor intensive. Changing regulatory pressures, rising medical costs and the increased costs of administering customer interactions is threatening the provider's ability to improve the quality of healthcare while reducing the cost of service.

As illustrated in Figure 5.11, IBM provides several solutions to address the needs of the Healthcare industry. The global healthcare industry is undergoing a major transformation, focusing on improving internal operations and reducing administrative and clinical costs. Additionally, healthcare is faced with pending government regulations, such as the Health Insurance Portability and Accountability Act (HIPAA), which mandates security and privacy practices.

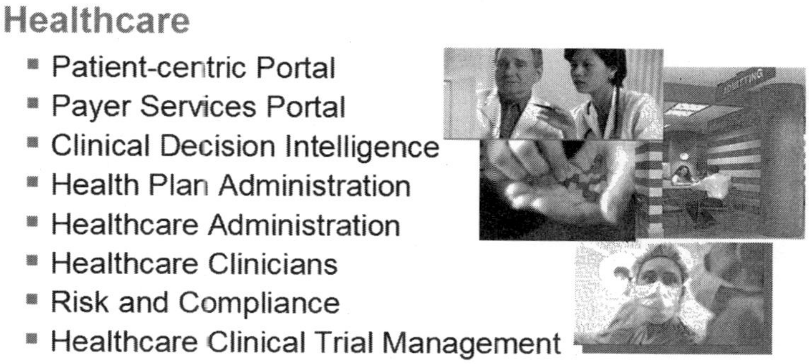

Figure 5.11. Healthcare industry solutions.

Finally, the aging population in the developed world and the continuous introduction of new medical technologies, drugs, and approaches to well-being add more layers of complexity.

The inability to provide clinicians and patients with real-time actionable data is a serious challenge and is caused because systems are unable to correlate data from multiple applications with different interfaces. Patient and clinical information input redundancies abound. Managing paper-based processes is hurting revenue cycles and causing inefficiencies. The inability to quickly find patient data, access relevant medical knowledge, and locate specialty practices or physicians causes life threatening delays. There need to be ways of providing patients secure access to schedule and view test results while protecting privacy and ensuring compliance with new government regulations, such as HIPAA regulations. When employees from clinical operations, process improvement, finance, and health information management join forces with physicians to reengineer processes, they need reliable business productivity tools to help them share information and collaborate.

IBM works closely with companies and organizations in the healthcare industry to understand the needs of this industry and provide solutions to address the challenges it faces. The Lotus Workplace software will provide different views of shared information to doctors, nurses, and administrators based on specific roles. And based on specific roles, training for staff on regulatory guidelines can be mapped out, provided, and tracked. Lotus Workplace improves patient flow with data collection and analysis tools, leading to improved quality of healthcare. The secure collaboration can be done in real time with people such as those in different practices, specialists, partners, and even patients. This improves overall communication and information flow. Patient records and clinical data can be made available to mobile healthcare provider staff.

The IBM Workplace family of products can enable doctors and nurses to have secure access to people, patient data, and business applications throughout the day using whatever access point they choose (mobile phone, computer, pager, etc.) without being tied to the office network. Healthcare IT departments can leverage investments in existing systems by using the operating system that is most efficient for their business. These solutions provide the ability to centrally manage clients from servers, dynamically provisioning upgrades to hospital staff members' desktops and mobile devices, and expanding the feature sets when required. Patient information can be protected and preserved with a higher level of security. Hospitals can improve patient satisfaction by allowing patients to schedule appointments and review test results online, and close communication gaps and improve patient management processes with customizable reporting tools. Improved response time to patient care needs results by moving from a paper-based or heterogeneous patient information system to shared information exchange.

Healthcare providers and payers are facing intensifying scrutiny by governments for possible fraud and abuse violations. Regulatory and accreditation bodies have also tightened operational requirements. An integrated, comprehensive compliance program is a necessity for today's healthcare organizations. The development and implementation of a compliance program is a major focus of most organizations involved with the healthcare industry. An organization will only be able to demonstrate that their compliance program is effective when the program has been integrated into the day-to-day operations of every department. An effective program creates an environment that reinforces the commitment to compliance while providing a framework to identify and correct potential issues of noncompliance. The compliance program should not impede or replace the organizational processes currently in place, but rather, compliment and enhance them in order to create a more effective and efficient operation. Workplace solutions provide the ability to address and measure effectiveness of regulatory compliance requirements across the healthcare organization with secure document management and auditable (virtual) paper trails.

The Healthcare Provider solution improves patient flow with data collection and analysis tools, leading to improved quality of healthcare for patients. It enables secure collaboration in real time with other practices, specialists, partners, and even patients, which improves overall communication and information flow. Patient records and clinical data can be made available to mobile healthcare provider staff. This will help close communication gaps and improve patient management processes with customizable reporting tools. It will provide key information to mobile healthcare professionals based on their information needs and role and provide the ability to make timely, cost-effective decisions based on the availability of information spanning multiple hospitals or clinics. This also will improve response time to patient care needs by moving from a paper-based or heterogeneous patient information system to shared information exchange. This solution centrally manages clients from servers, dynamically provisioning upgrades to hospital staff members' desktops and mobile devices, and expanding feature sets when required. It protects and preserves patient documents with a higher level of security, with authentication at the local and server level, thus enabling extranet access that includes patient self-service access. This also provides the ability to address and measure effectiveness of regulatory compliance requirements across the healthcare organization with secure document management and auditable (virtual) paper trails. For example, this will assist in addressing HIPAA privacy regulations relating to patient registration and data access with secure, centralized data store of documents.

The Healthcare Collaborative Network solution addresses the problems related to inefficient exchange of information between providers and insurers. This solution provides a foundation for detection and rapid response to adverse healthcare events. It creates a network that enables private and secure transmission of healthcare data and can also help healthcare providers improve the quality of patient care while reducing costs associated with government reporting requirements and technical integration. Key benefits are improved hospital business and IT operations efficiency, integrated processes, and reduced administrative costs.

The Healthcare Patient-centric Portal solution addresses the problems related to the lack of coordinated information about a patient's clinical care. This solution provides accelerated integration of disparate applications to improve the availability of integrated clinical information to clinicians. This secure solution enables a user-friendly interface to patient data across clinical systems. Key benefits are improved quality and safety of care, improved staff productivity due to minimized training time, application/information integration from a customer view, and increased clinician satisfaction and utilization of IT systems.

The Healthcare Clinical Decision Intelligence solution addresses the problems related to the lack of a consolidated repository for patient data and increased time in making clinical diagnosis and treatment. This solution provides in-depth prospective and retrospective data analysis by aggregating data from multiple disparate applications. It can help to decrease time to clinical diagnosis and treatment, and reduce the safety risks posed by a lack of information. Benefits are improved workflows, straight-through processing, process monitoring, and reduced processing costs.

The Healthcare Payer Services Portal solution addresses the problem of inefficient customer service processes. This solution is designed to help make business and IT operations more efficient by providing a single point of access to key systems, organization, customer information, and collaboration tools. It offers reduced administration costs through a consistent role-based interface with single sign-on that helps to minimize the learning curve, a secure framework allowing employees to access applications anywhere at any time, and collaborative and workflow capabilities to streamline and speed business processes. Key benefits are improved workflow, ease of doing business, an integrated customer view, and the potential for increased market share.

The Healthcare Health Plan Administration solution addresses the problems related to high administrative costs in manual plan-administration processes. This solution provides payers with an effective means to leverage information to support decision making based on health outcomes data. The solution also allows payers to manage continued demand for information and analyses to support new incentive-based provider reimbursement and consumer demands for access to health benefit, financial, disease, and treatment information. Key benefits are improved administration and cost reduction through automated adjudication, improved workflow, and streamlined processes, as well as improved business relationships with employer/government sponsors, plan members, business partners, sales channels, and regulatory organizations.

Insurance

In the insurance industry, operational improvements are fuelling the drive to be better at serving customers' needs and sharpen the competitive edge within the insurance industry. Insurers want to address key operational challenges, including underwriting performance, claims cost management, and optimizing the use of reinsurance. They want better ways of attracting quality people and retaining them. They aim for closer control of risk aggregation.

As illustrated in Figure 5.12, IBM provides several solutions to address the needs of the Insurance industry. They need better business productivity solutions and adoption of such by their employees so they can foster an environment of creativity and so they can do things like collaborate with various participants and figure out more appropriate reinsurance programs. There is a strong willingness to innovate. Many organizations face the dilemma of how to instill tighter underwriting discipline without stifling the flexibility and entrepreneurial flair that are central to the insurance industry's success. They also need to be better able to manage the business through the next downturn.

Figure 5.12. Insurance industry solutions.

Insurance provides protection for risks that an individual or company cannot afford to run. It works by having a group of individuals or companies pay money, as premiums, to a central fund. This fund is used to provide compensation, or claim payments, to individuals or companies that incur damage or loss to their person or possessions.

The insurance industry typically organizes insurance offerings into two segments. The first segment is life and asset management, which includes pensions, life insurance, and investments. The second is property and casualty, which includes motor, household, aviation, marine, and healthcare.

The IBM Integrated Claims Management insurance solution addresses the problems related to having manual, inefficient, lengthy claims management processes. This solution is designed to help insurers increase claims efficiency and effectiveness by managing the complete claims cycle. Through mobility, automation, and process integration, the solution provides insurers with the capabilities to improve cycle time, increase fraud detection, and improve their loss ratios. Key benefits are automated adjudication, enhanced customer satisfaction, delivery of quality information, an enhanced overall image of the company, and decreased settlement time and cost. The IBM Integrated Claims Management insurance solution provides consistent access to a customized view of the system based upon the claim user's role and responsibility. It provides mobile and collaborative tools to extend the reach and range of claim users both inside and outside the enterprise. It makes it possible to capture, store, and retrieve all structured and nonstructured data. The solution provides secure access to policy holder information across the enterprise and the ability to integrate all parties internally and externally associated with the claims process

(B2B and B2C). It automates workflow driven by business rules and enabled by monitoring tools to track the process and adjust as required over time.

The IBM Integrated Underwriting insurance solution helps achieve a decrease in underwriting costs and enables a company to respond to a changing business environment more effectively. This solution is designed to help insurers improve their underwriting capacity and productivity by providing integration and establishment of a disciplined approach to underwriting. The solution provides a secure role-based workplace using process collaborations, document management, and integration of information. The IBM Integrated Underwriting insurance solution helps insurers effectively determine pending requirements, access underwriting information to assess risk, and dispose and issue policies using business-rules-based workflow tools to manage submission, renewals, policy issuance, document management, and key performance indicators. Key benefits are increased underwriting efficiency, better underwriting decisions, increased agent/agency retention, and enhanced underwriting performance through the ability to react to changes in business environment (risks and exposures).

The Insurance Policy Management solution addresses the problems related to having manual, out-of-date, inflexible policy administration systems and technologies. This solution provides insurers with capabilities to reduce the cost of administration and streamline processes by modernizing and transforming their back office. It offers a secure integrated work environment, including document management, workflow integration, and business process management. These capabilities provide a flexible and integrated work environment to manage the policy administration process. The IBM Workplace component integrates the multiple supporting internal applications and external service provider information to manage processes such as endorsements, system entry, payment collection, and commission payments. Key benefits are increased premiums and customer retention, enhanced customer satisfaction, reduced expenses, enhanced quality, and improved efficiency.

The IBM Channel Distribution Integration insurance solution addresses the problems related to having multiple channels, high customer churn, declining premiums, and manual channel management processes. Insurers are challenged with effectively providing customers a single brand experience across many access points, enabling the enterprise to recognize and react to a customer appropriately at each access point. The IBM Channel Distribution Integration insurance solution is designed to help an insurer seamlessly integrate and manage its channels and service areas, including agents, call centers, contact centers, and Internet sales and service channels. Accessibility to insured information is made available through portal and/or mobility solutions for channels requiring direct access to agent/broker services (such as customer information or insured policy status) or to back-end financial management (commissions, sales and marketing, and agent rating and scoring). Using IBM's B2B capabilities (ACORD compliant) and ISV relationships, the IBM Channel Distribution Integration insurance solution provides agents, insurers and reinsurers SEMCI (Single-Entry Multiple Company Interface) capabilities to help improve transaction efficiencies and reduce operational costs. Key benefits are increased productivity of distribution channels, increased speed of processing customer transactions, reduced overall servicing costs, and delivery of a seamless experience to the customer.

The Insurance Customer Insight solution addresses the problems related to achieving a customer-centric view across multiple channels and product lines. This solution enables an insurer to establish a customer-focused strategy with supporting technology around campaign management, sales automation, a single customer view of information, and customer analysis and segmentation. The solution provides an insurer with the organizational strategy and analytical modeling tools to provide customer lifetime values, propensity scores, wallet shares, producer metrics, and other profitability factors. Benefits of this solution include improved customer satisfaction through a "one company, one voice" strategy, customer touch-point differentiation, and improved cross-selling/upselling capabilities.

Life Sciences

The business challenges of a pharmaceutical company today include the ability to be more flexible and establish and maintain "real-time" relationships with everyone in the value chain, including regulators, healthcare providers, and physicians. Companies try to capture and maximize all research, discovery, and development processes for new drugs, minimizing risks associated with staff changes. Many have goals such as to establish and implement best practices for bringing new drugs from conception to consumption, automate the new drug approval (NDA) process, which is traditionally a paper-based system, and accelerate the time to market for new drugs.

As illustrated in Figure 5.13, IBM provides several solutions to address the needs of the Life Sciences industry. To serve their customers and value chain community better, these companies need to improve their brand image by providing a single, integrated look into the company on products, partnerships, community education, etc. To be a worldwide success, they need to act globally by efficiently and effectively communicating to one or many, whoever they are, whatever they do, wherever they are located.

Life Sciences

- Clinical Trials & Management
- Annotation & Knowledge Sharing
- Clinical Genomics
- Investigator Recruitment & Trials Mgmt
- HR Management
- Corporate Information Asset Management
- Compliance in a Regulated Environment

Figure 5.13. Life Sciences industry solutions.

The life sciences industry enters the on demand era when as a new cancer drug prepares to enter clinical trials, the lead scientist downloads three years' worth of findings directly into the pharmaceutical company's database with the push of a button. This data automatically generates customized patient recruitment profiles, which are forwarded to the head of patient recruitment. The head of regulatory controls restructures his group, realizing now that he'll need only a single employee to handle the FDA submission.

There is an explosion of data facing researchers throughout the life sciences industry. IBM solutions can help turn this data into scientific discovery, streamline drug development processes, and develop new treatment delivery systems. In addition, these solutions can help effectively manage massive data sets and accelerate the pace of drug discovery and development, and can aid users to address regulations, share patient data, develop targeted treatments, and improve the quality of diagnostic decisions.

The Workplace solutions enable a standards-based portal that simplifies the integration of existing business applications. Faster drug approval processes can be achieved with a shared documents repository supported by search and workflow engines.

The Life Sciences Corporate Information Asset Management solution addresses the problems related to enabling data access and management across multiple sources with inconsistent security standards and formats, and to meeting FDA CFR 21-11 guidelines and the ever-increasing volumes of such data. This solution delivers secure storage and processing of life sciences documentation and data records. It provides a records management environment that addresses the needs for the storage, search/retrieval, long-term archiving, and disaster recovery of data, documents, analytical results, and e-mail messages generated in the pharmaceutical process—from discovery through manufacturing and delivery. Key benefits are improved workflow, streamlined access to information, increased security, and risk management to assist with regulatory compliance.

The Life Sciences Investigator Recruitment and Trials Management solution addresses investigator recruitment/retainment and successful and efficient trials management. This solution provides an integrated, portal-based environment for investigator access. It is designed to increase the effectiveness and productivity of clinical trials by bringing together learning modules, investigator resources, collaboration capabilities, and access to applications. Key benefits are more educated investigator teams, automated recruitment, and increased investigator collaboration.

The Life Sciences Clinical Genomics solution addresses the challenges related to the study of the genetic origins of common diseases for development and delivery of targeted treatment solutions, which requires management and analysis of large volumes of diverse, heterogeneous data types. This solution provides an environment for capturing clinical patient data for reuse as the basis for directed drug development research. By offering data aggregation and streamlined access, the solution is designed to meet the challenge of accessing and analyzing increasing amounts of life sciences data. Key benefits are improved capture and integration of patient data, increased process efficiency, and improved reuse of clinical data to drive research.

The Life Sciences Clinical Trials Management solution addresses the problems related to the lack of consistency of information, multiple interfaces, process delays, and compliance with CFR 21-11 guidelines. This solution helps life sciences organizations manage time-critical information; documents; budgets; schedules of investigators, patients, and clinical trial staff; and all related components of a clinical trial. It can be used to integrate the clinical trials management process with the FDA submission document process needed to satisfy government compliance regulations for documents and processes in a validated environment. Key benefits are reduced and managed risk, improved workflow, increased clinical trials efficiency, and reduced errors.

The Life Sciences Annotations and Knowledge Sharing solution addresses the problem related to the inability to capture tacit knowledge and to share and collaborate. This solution allows a life sciences organization to use annotations to qualify data entry and interpretation. The solution also provides a collaborative environment for sharing knowledge, expertise, and ideas. Insights, which then point to subsets of data used for analysis, can be identified based on annotated content, metadata, and authorship. Key benefits are improved creation of document annotations, increased security of annotation storage, and improved ability to share and search for annotated content.

Retail

Consumers today are more knowledgeable, savvy, and self-sufficient and are less loyal. Their relationships with retailers are driven by three things: time, value, and information. For retailers of every size, in every segment, the challenge is to deliver a superior customer shopping experience.

IBM has worked with many retail industry organizations to understand the unique retail industry requirements. IBM has several solutions that address the problems retail companies face.

Retail chains, which may have hundreds of specialty outlets in many locations, always strive to provide more value to customers and be the most cost effective at doing such. Promotions to move high inventory products must be effectively communicated frequently, results tracked and reported, statistics gathered and shared between participating outlets and headquarters. Inventories must be monitored and managed. Customers may order online or go to an outlet, and the two channel systems need to be integrated to maximize fulfillment productivity. Getting timely actionable information to headquarters in order to make effective promotional decisions can be challenging.

As illustrated in Figure 5.14, IBM provides several solutions to address the needs of the Retail industry.

Employees in remote outlet locations need to be aware of promotions that customers going into the store may have read about in a promotional advertisement. Often these kinds of communications are handled through traditional ways, such as headquarters sending e-mails to store managers, who print off the notices and pass out to employees. Giving every employee a desktop computer to access e-mail and corporate applications is too costly to provide to store sales staff. A kiosk browser-based solution is needed.

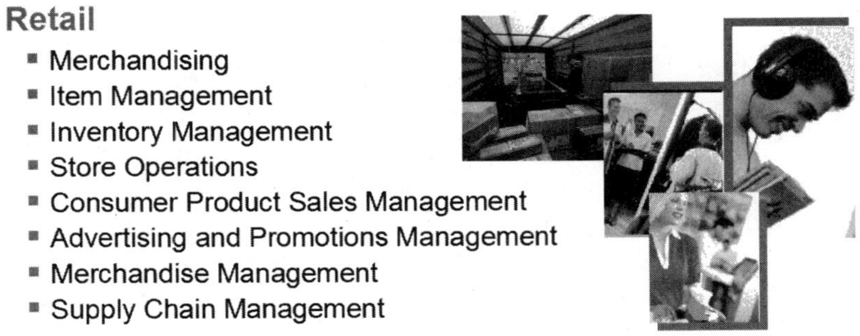

Figure 5.14. Retail industry solutions.

In the retail industry it is common to have high employee and store management turnover. This necessitates the need for ongoing new-employee training and a system for job role-based educational guidance.

Significant productivity gains an demployee satisfaction improvements can be achieved by implementing solutions built by IBM Workplace products. As illustrated in Figure 5.15, providing Web browser-based or rich client e-mail and application access to employees enables them to share information whether connected or not, provide personalized views of shared corporate information based on roles, and integrate business applications and information within the online work environment. Management would be better able to monitor critical business metrics with online reporting tools and alerts. Retail businesses could provide role-based training to employees faster and more cost effectively—and at each employee's unique schedule and pace.

Awareness capabilities help provide instant access to experts across the retail chain and enable sales staff to receive information alerts on promos and other offers instantly. Built-in editors are sufficient for many users, eliminating the need to provide everyone with the same complete (expensive) personal productivity suites.

Employees can find information faster by having a single location containing company and personal information, including store headlines, employee benefits, store performance versus store plans, district view for forecasting and

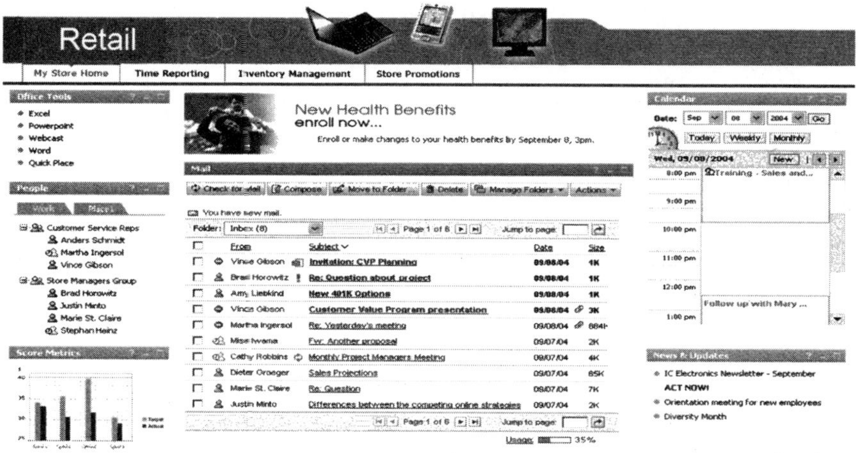

Figure 5.15. Retail employee Workplace user environment.

planning, corporate view with aggregated business performance data/modeling, and inventory tracking, allowing them to work more efficiently.

The Retail Merchandising solution helps address the problem of getting the right product on the shelves at the right price all the time. This solution enables retailers to reduce inventory carrying costs through better inventory management, improve supplier performance and accountability by measuring service level agreements and compliance, and improve gross margin and sales by quickly analyzing early sales data of new products and short lifecycle items. The solution enables retailers to increase merchandising effectiveness by consolidating information from disparate sources such as the point-of-sale transaction log, historical buying data, and a vendor scorecard, and by providing this single up-to-date view of critical information to the merchandising organization. Key benefits are increased sales by maximizing in-stock percentages, increased customer service through on-time order fulfillment, and protected margins by minimizing markdowns.

The Retail Item Management solution helps to maximize in-stock percentages and reduce manual errors/delays in product information management. This solution provides retailers with a fully automated and integrated set of data synchronization and product-information-management processes to streamline the supply chain. The solution helps retailers reduce the cost per SKU by eliminating manual processes and the errors caused by them, and by allowing companies to seamlessly trade item information with their suppliers. Key benefits are reduced supply chain costs, reduced purchase order errors, accelerated time to market, effective supplier collaboration, and reduced stock-outs.

The Retail Advertising, Marketing and Promotions solution addresses the problems related to rising print advertising costs, digital asset management, and ineffective promotions. This solution enables retailers to design and execute effective advertising (dynamic digital merchandising) and promotion plans. Using IBM and partner software, retailers can develop a deeper understanding of target customers and provide advertising and promotions that are aligned to these customers' wants and needs, in order to drive traffic into stores, generate a higher percentage of purchases, and provide a higher return on the promotional and advertising investment. Key benefits are increased promotional return on investment, sales, customer loyalty, and market share.

The Retail Inventory Management solution addresses the problems related to tracking inventory through the warehouse and distribution system. This solution provides retailers with a standards-based solution that enables them to implement RFID technology within their enterprise and integrate it with their current inventory management processes. This solution helps retailers improve supply chain efficiencies through tracking and tracing capabilities and automated document matching processes. Key benefits are automated tracking and tracking of inventory, reduced excess inventory, reduced shrinkage, and decreased inventory costs.

The Retail Store Operations solution addresses the problems related to the inability to capture and track orders from all sources, point-to-point interfaces, and an inflexible architecture for integrating across multiple channels. This solution enables retailers to run their store effectively and efficiently through expert managers, optimized labor management, and well-managed inventory. Using this solution, retailers can leverage computing, database, and business-activity monitoring technologies to deliver a true real-time, integrated store application infrastructure that provides inventory tracking and improves employee and store manager productivity, all at an affordable price. These capabilities reduce labor costs so that retailers can focus their capital on their core business, and reduce employee inefficiencies so that in-store labor can focus on revenue-generating activities.

IBM Workplace for Retail Store Operations

IBM Workplace for Retail Store Operations provides the ability to monitor business metrics, define, schedule and monitor in-store tasks, consistently deploy in-store promotions, perform self-service human resources tasks as well as take and deploy innovative learning modules. IBM Workplace for Retail Store Operations provides the ability to increase operations effectiveness and efficiency, employee and customer satisfaction, and subsequently drive additional revenue.

Retailers are now focusing more on in-store capability as the next step to gaining advantage. In-store operations are plagued by high employee turnover rates and lack of access to timely operational information. Retail store managers and associates must be able to quickly and efficiently plan and execute their store's day-to-day operations.

This solution can help retailers provide more efficient, responsive shops. They can increase productivity by streamlining all non-sales and sales activities with focus on value-added activities. This assists in reducing training costs while making individuals more effective, and filling skills and knowledge gaps. It lower costs and improves employee satisfaction by providing self-service options. It will help improve decision making by leveraging collective know-how across and outside the organization. And it will drive overall employee productivity through greater self-management, empowerment, and education. This will enable sales associates to master new products and customer selling skills through timely and effective e-learning without requiring time away from their jobs.

WebSphere Portal for Retail Supply Chain

The retail industry faces many challenges. It is in a state of continuous flux with unpredictable growth. But growth can come from better managing business processes more than from clever advertising or even from better products. IBM WebSphere Portal for Retail Supply Chain helps provide greater focus on the supply chain process, delivering business capabilities key to decreasing costs, accessing trading partners, and rapidly providing product to the consumer. This is for on demand businesses of all sizes that need to connect the right people with the right information to increase business responsiveness and to mitigate risks. Retailers improve supply chain execution, and drive growth with new portal offerings.

This helps improve communications with trading partners, stores, and distribution centers. It creates access to partners and suppliers to confirm product assortment, pricing, and promotions. It helps control costs by improving the methods for buying material, components, and finished goods and can provide a reduction in process lead time with an improvement in "time to shelf."

WebSphere Portal for Retail Supply Chain reduces administrative tasks in merchandising, buying, property, finance and store operations which can all lead to a decrease in costs. It increases visibility of stock sales, waste, and consumer demand throughout the supply chain. This facilitates collaboration and communication for improving relationships with suppliers and encouraging greater participation in auctions. This helps execute promotions more rapidly, decreasing time to ship and remove underperforming products from the shelves.

Telecommunications

As companies in the telecom industry work to regain the confidence of investors and comply with new regulatory requirements, such as those imposed by the Sarbanes-Oxley Act in the United States, many are making efforts to provide better information, invest in technologies that will enable better productivity, and provide the ever-increasing demands of their customers. Improvements in business intelligence and integration technologies can help telecom corporations by giving them a real-time view of operations and allowing executives to make decisions more quickly and effectively.

The telecommunications companies control the networks that will enable the highway of the on demand journey. From outsourcing, to grid computing, and to the integration of galaxies of partners, suppliers, and customers, these things will all go through the wires and wireless spectrum controlled by the industry.

As illustrated in Figure 5.16, IBM provides several solutions to address the needs of the Telecommunications industry. The industry itself will reap the benefits from going on demand. On demand is a powerful way to combat the product substitution, the customer churn, and worst of all the islands of automation that are eroding the industry's margins and causing it great pain. To put it simply, the telecom value chain runs from suppliers to networks to operations to customer that are all connected and upheld by enterprise management. Three key parts of the telecom value chain are customer relationships, network operations, and the supply chain. IBM has worked with most telecom providers and industry organizations to understand the needs of this industry and develop solutions that will address the key problems experienced.

The Telecommunications Partner Content Enabler solution addresses the problems related to long, costly new product introduction cycles, limited "killer apps" to create customer lock-in, and high customer churn. This solution allows an ISP (Internet service provider) to manage and automate the new product introduction cycle of sell-through revenue opportunities, such as ring tones, games, multimedia content, and business applications. Key benefits are reduced time to market for new products and services, more flexible and effective product management, and increased revenue opportunities.

The Telecommunications Contact Center Optimizer solution addresses the problems related to rising customer support costs, high customer churn, and being able to give customers "what they want, when they want it, how they want it." This solution offers an environment for Internet service providers to

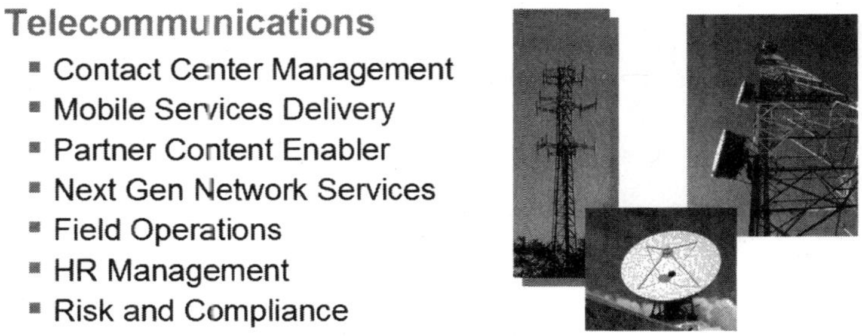

Figure 5.16. Telecommunications industry solutions.

allow end customers to select their communication medium of choice (phone, IVR, voice, mobile, Web, e-mail) for account self-service. Key benefits are improved customer service, reduced support costs, and lower customer churn.

The Telecommunications Mobile Services Delivery solution addresses the problem of wanting to improve employee productivity with improved up-to-date information. This solution allows ISPs to extend seamless connectivity and unified support to the enterprise. It helps them enable their mobile workforce regardless of geography, access point, or device type while also empowering the enterprise to include customized value-added services, such as portals and applications. Key benefits are new revenue opportunities, enterprise customer focus, and creation of long-term value-added service opportunities.

The Telecommunications Next Generation Network Services solution addresses the problems related to the evolution to soft-switch networks, which requires huge software infrastructure changes. This solution provides comprehensive, high-performance business application servers and development tools to enable faster time to market and lower costs. It can enable a subscriber management portal for provisioning next-generation network services, such as video-on-demand, increased high-speed connectivity demand, and revenue through personalized services. Providers could experience increases in customer satisfaction through value-added services and reduced administrative costs through centralized management of subscriptions.

The Telecommunications OSS/BSS Optimization solution addresses the problems related to the lack of centralized information across heterogeneous application infrastructure at the BSS/OSS layer: slower response to customer and market demands. This solution enables ISPs to integrate processes across systems in a cost-effective, flexible manner while continuously optimizing enterprise processes and the corresponding IT infrastructure. The integration of business and IT helps to lower operational costs while increasing revenue. Key benefits of the solution are optimization of assets, cost reduction, and increased company-wide efficiency and flexibility.

About the Authors

Ron Sebastian
Senior IT Consultant
IBM Software Group

Douglas W. Spencer
Program Director,
IBM Software Group

Ron and Doug have worked together on various projects with IBM during the past 15 years. In the late 1980s, they were first teamed together as members of one of the first software group teams within IBM Canada. They developed and delivered full day technical briefings on topics such as application development, client/server database, and client/server systems management.

In 1994, Ron and Doug moved to Singapore to form a company which provided client server consulting throughout Asia. Contracted back to IBM Asia, they were part of a technical SWAT team supporting IBM software throughout Asia Pacific.

Ron returned to North America in 1996. Doug continued in Asia and then the Middle East. In 2000, Doug teamed back up with Ron and moved to New York to work together as part of an Executive Briefing team. Doug is currently the Program Director of that team, now called "IBM Software Live!" Ron is currently the Technical Assistant to the Vice President of Development in the Lotus Software Division.

Ron Sebastian
Senior Consultant, Lotus Development

Ron has been with IBM for 27 years and is currently the Technical Assistant to the Vice President of Development in the Lotus Software Division. In this position, Ron performs technical product and technology evaluations, represents the development team in critical customer situations, and delivers external and internal technology presentations.

Over the years, Ron has worked with customers to define and implement their e-business architecture and applications around the world. Ron has extensive experience in implementing client/server solutions in both North America and Asia. In Singapore, as the IBM Software Sales Team Leader for the Southern Asia Pacific region, he was responsible for advising IBM customers in the area of client/server computing and assisting in the development of technical strategies to address their business requirements. He was involved in several IBM Consulting projects throughout the Asia Pacific region.

Prior to this, Ron was a Senior Technical Instructor for IBM Education Services where he developed and delivered course material in a broad area of IBM Software products including OS/2, LAN Server, application development and AIX. Ron started his career with IBM as a Communications Specialist in the Data Processing (DP) Division supporting the banking industry.

Ron was raised in Hamilton, Canada. He is a graduate of Mohawk College of Applied Arts and Technology with an honors diploma in Control Systems Technology with a specialty in micro electronics. He currently resides in Ancaster, Ontario, Canada.

Douglas W. Spencer
Worldwide Program Director
IBM Software Group

With over 19 years' experience with IBM, Doug is currently the Program Director of the worldwide executive briefing team called "IBM Software Live!" (formerly "e-business Live!"). The team delivers full day briefings with live demonstrations and presentations showing the depth and breadth of the IBM software portfolio.

Doug was born and raised in Toronto, Canada. He graduated from Seneca College of Applied Arts and Technology, in Toronto, after studying Computing Programming and Analysis, DP Audit Major.

Beginning his career at IBM Canada as a programmer co-op student and hired full-time in 1988, Doug became part of an IBM internal support center providing internal systems support, developing and conducting educational training on mainframe applications, PC operating systems and software applications.

Doug was teamed up with Ron Sebastian in 1989. The two combined skills to develop technical briefings which not only presented technical computing concepts, but also demonstrated them. The approach was effective and well received.

Doug has extensive international experience. During his career he has worked in Canada, USA, Asia-Pacific, Europe, Middle East and Africa regions. Doug has experience with a wide range of cross platform, international, and cross industry software solutions. He has managed technical sales teams, technical services teams, and had several regional leadership responsibilities.

Doug is the author of three editions of a reference book titled, "IBM Software Guide for e-business," written in 1998 and 1999. He is also the author of a recently published book titled, "IBM Software for e-business on demand." In recent years, Doug presented in and produced several interactive video CDs, which are a video capture of the briefing program content he and his team deliver worldwide.

Doug's time in Asia had him based in Singapore for over two years, the Philippines for half a year, and Malaysia for one year working as a contractor for IBM. In 1998 and 1999, Doug was based in Dubai, United Arab Emirates, working directly for IBM EMEA and providing technical sales support on IBM software throughout the Middle East and Africa. Since 2000, Doug has joined IBM USA working on teams based out of Somers, NY.

Index

Reader Feedback Sheet

Your comments and suggestions are very important in shaping future publications. Please e-mail us at *moreinfo@maxpress.com* or photocopy this page, jot down your thoughts, and fax it to (850) 934-9981 or mail it to:

Maximum Press

Attn: Jim Hoskins

605 Silverthorn Road

Gulf Breeze, FL 32561

Exploring IBM @server zSeries and S/390 Servers, Eighth Edition
by Jim Hoskins and Bob Frank
464 pages
$59.95
ISBN: 1-885068-91-3

Exploring IBM @server xSeries, Twelfth Edition
by Jim Hoskins, Bill Wilson, and Ray Winkel
208 pages
$49.95
ISBN: 1-885068-83-2

Marketing with E-mail, Third Edition
by Shannon Kinnard
352 pages
$29.95
ISBN: 1-885068-68-9

Marketing on the Internet, Sixth Edition
by Jan Zimmerman
488 pages
$34.95
ISBN: 1-885068-80-8

Business-to-Business Internet Marketing, Fourth Edition
by Barry Silverstein
432 pages
$34.95
ISBN: 1-885068-72-7

101 Ways to Promote Your Web Site, Fifth Edition
by Susan Sweeney, C.A.
488 pages
$29.95
ISBN: 1-931644-21-7

101 Internet Businesses You Can Start From Home
by Susan Sweeney, C.A.
520 pages
$29.95
ISBN: 1-885068-59-X

Internet Marketing for Less Than $500/Year, Second Edition
by Marcia Yudkin
352 pages
$29.95
ISBN: 1-885068-69-7

To purchase a Maximum Press book, visit your local bookstore
or call 1-800-989-6733 (US/Canada) or 1-850-934-4583 (International)
online ordering available at ***www.maxpress.com***